# *Courageous Leadership*

## Identify & Achieve Your Lifetime Goals

### *A 12-Week Action Plan*

**By**
**J.R. Flatter, Ph.D.**

**Version 1.0 Published May 6, 2018**

**DISCLAIMER AND TERMS OF USE AGREEMENT**
The author and publisher of this book/eBook and the accompanying materials have used their best efforts in preparing this book/eBook. The author and publisher make no representation or warranties with respect to the accuracy, applicability, fitness, or completeness of the contents of this book/eBook. The information contained in this book/eBook is strictly for educational purposes. Therefore, if you wish to apply ideas contained in this book/eBook, you are taking full responsibility for your actions.

*Brian,*

*Thank you for your friendship across the years! I hope you & your Proteges enjoy the book.*

*S/F*

## Contributors

I am a firm advocate of Ralph Waldo Emerson's statement that we learn from everyone we meet. Thus, everyone I have ever met has contributed to this book in some form or fashion. However, even with that belief, I would be remiss if I did not mention a few of the book's direct contributors:

Mr. James Adams who expertly, and often painfully, allowed me to give explicit form and shape to this philosophy.

Ms. Cynthia Gremban-Barnaby who took control of our motley crew and skillfully led us to completion.

Mr. Lucas Flatter who took time away from his game design and cartooning career to apply his many talents to the look and feel of the book.

I dedicate this book to my wife, Alicia for she has been and remains the guiding hand behind any and all courageous actions I have taken during our life together. Without her patience and love, I would otherwise have certainly pursued my various excesses to an early mortality.

# Table of Contents

# CHAPTER 1:

## INTRODUCTION

*Courage is not simply one of the virtues, but the form of every virtue at the testing point*
-C.S. Lewis

The renowned scholar and author C.S. Lewis accurately captures in his statement that ***Courage*** is the foundation upon which all other leadership characteristics stand. This simple yet profound declaration is the "Big T" truth upon which this book is founded.

***Courageous Leadership*** is the demonstrated willingness & ability to communicate and accomplish specific goals & objectives for self, others, and organizations while adhering to a unique combination of technical, cognitive, & emotional ***courage characteristics***. Learning, accepting, developing, and demonstrating these characteristics is the major purpose of this book.

The ***Courageous Leader*** has chosen to live an exceptional life – consciously assigning themselves actions and goals that are uncommon to most others. The ***Courageous Leader*** – by choosing to be the exception – is neither surprised nor discouraged by the fact that they are usually the only one in the room with such lofty ideals. The ***Courageous Leader*** recognizes they are imperfect – yet feels an obligation to lead themselves and others towards excellence – despite their human shortcomings.

This book is about ***developing*** your leadership knowledge, skills, abilities, & experiences (KSA&E). Given these developmental objectives, it will first introduce you to the potentially life-changing philosophy of ***Courageous Leadership***. Then, as leadership development requires much more than simply reading inspirational quotes and inspiring stories, this book will also guide you through 12 weeks of developmental action which will re-invent the way you think, behave, communicate, and lead!

Concurrently, and perhaps even more importantly, you will either draft for the first time or further clarify and then begin executing your Lifetime Goals & Objectives. These goals & objectives will become the *purpose* for which you pursue Courageous Leadership. They will become the *purpose* of your life. And these goals & objectives will be enabled by your achievement and demonstration of the Courageous Leadership Characteristics.

In the end, if you do the work and accept the accompanying roles and responsibilities, you will be transformed into a proficient *Courageous Leader* – on a lifelong path toward Mastery.

In my own life and leadership, I strive to be a *Courageous Leader* – but I remain far from the ideal leader this book identifies. Thus, my intent is not to set myself up on a pedestal as the *Courageous Leader* you should ascribe to be. Rather, my intent is to show you – through the knowledge and experiences I have gained through 40+ years of leading myself, others, and organizations; studying and writing about leadership; and teaching and consulting on leadership – a clear path to your own life as a *Courageous Leader*.

Per the laws of physics, it takes a person just under 1.5 seconds to dive from the top of a ten-meter diving tower. But I can tell you from experience, having done the leap on numerous occasions, this quick drop feels like an eternity. As a novice, once you step from the ledge, you have no control over direction; little control over whether you enter the water vertical or horizontal; and no control over the speed and energy of impact. But the first time you jump is the hardest. The developmental exercises in this book are designed to be figurative, controlled, risk-free jumps from the ten-meter ledge – again and again – during the twelve weeks. As you move from Awareness; to Familiarity; and then Proficiency – while identifying a life-long path toward Mastery, you will take the dive countless times – each progressively less frightening and more informed than the other.

And each leap, whether figurative or literal, requires increased courage. As we start this journey together, I want to make it perfectly clear that an absence of such courage is not cowardice –

rather, it is simply a life of normalcy. Normal people do voluntarily jump from ten-meter towers; normal people do not burn for evermore responsibility; normal people do not have an innate drive that requires they purposefully balance work, family, & self; and normal people do not voluntarily strive to go above and beyond on a daily basis. By picking up this book, I am assuming you already feel such a spark of courage within yourself. Further, you are willing to accept the challenges of living an exceptional life. And you are looking for assistance in identifying, executing, and sustaining a life-long plan to achieve such *Courageous Leadership*.

This book is focused on achieving *Courageous Leadership* "proficiency" – which is a step above "Familiarity" and a gigantic step below Mastery. Courageous Leadership Mastery is achieved over a lifetime of continual development and sustainment similar to the commitment required to achieve mastery in sports or music. Proficiency represents your ability to capably execute the courageous leadership characteristics.

Leadership as a field of research is only about 100 years old. In the early days, the field's scholars focused on "Great Men" – the Washingtons, the Lincolns, the Eisenhowers – to discern what we could *mimic* from them to apply to our own leadership. Over time, we've discovered that leadership is actually a set of technical, cognitive, and emotional *characteristics* that can be *learned and practiced* successfully by almost anyone. We have also discovered that achieving those competencies – in both individuals and organizations – is best achieved through a program of leadership development – hence the program format of this book. Of course, some people are born with innate talent and/or possess increased learning capacity but, at the end of the day, all of us can learn to dribble a basketball or pluck a guitar string.

Finally, I lead and teach people from all walks of life – across all levels of experience from CEOs to Entry-Level; across all fields of profession from Blue Collar to White Collar; and across all levels of education from Ph.D.'s to GED's. Thus, the 12-week path to *Courageous Leadership* proficiency identified in this book is relevant across those same demographics.

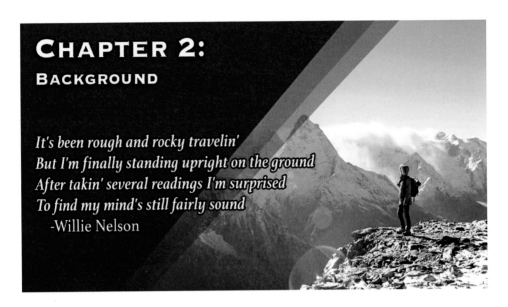

# CHAPTER 2:
## BACKGROUND

*It's been rough and rocky travelin'*
*But I'm finally standing upright on the ground*
*After takin' several readings I'm surprised*
*To find my mind's still fairly sound*
-Willie Nelson

As I rode my bicycle this morning, I laughed aloud with this Willie Nelson song humming in my mind; alone at dawn on a deserted country road; celebrating the simple fact that I was alive; and able to ride my bicycle 50 miles. For, looking back on my life thus far, it is apparent to me how fortunate I have been.

I was born on a small plot of land in the northeastern corner of Washington State. We called our home a "farm," but the only things that grew with much success on the steep hills and jagged rocks were children; as my parents eventually had seven of us in the decade between their teens and twenties. In addition to our small herd of children, we had two dogs; a milk cow; her yearly calf; a dozen chickens; and a few rabbits. It was the kind of place that was perfect for raising a family but fell far short of self-sufficiency. Until I was eight years old, our home was a tar-paper shack in a town of fewer than 250 people.

Children don't know they are poor. It's only after you are grown that clues begin to present themselves – such as my fond memories of riding atop my toy fire engine from one side of our house to the other – with the bare wood floor so uneven that I could easily coast the entire length with my feet sticking out to the sides. Or going to sleep in our living room on a fold-out couch, cuddled up with my younger brother for warmth, in a room that was so cold you could clearly see your breath. Or sleeping outside in the summer to avoid the heat – seeing the coyote's eyes in the dark staring attentively back at us.

A very nice lady came to visit us at one point when I was eight years old – to conduct what in hindsight was a health and welfare inspection – and thereby promptly recommended to her state agency that we move out of our "unacceptable" country home or be dispersed into foster care. Ironically, we were moved into a house just within the boundaries of a 150,000-person city that was dirtier and more dangerous than was our shack on the farm. Our new "home" was at the intersection of two four-lane streets running east to west and north to south – which hummed with heavy traffic at all hours of the day. Across the street on one side was a thirty-track railroad switching yard in which trains were constantly starting, stopping, and transiting through. Wandering homeless men – called hoboes in the language of the day – were frequent visitors either begging for food, sleeping in our truck, or asking for temporary work. Although it is almost cliché to say, we quite literally had to walk two miles to school in each direction – through some pretty rough neighborhoods. More than once, I arrived at school with torn clothing and a bloody nose from engaging in fist-fights along the route.

And I let everyone know how displeased I was in my new surroundings – parents, teachers, relatives, brothers, and sisters alike. As a fourth-grader in the country, I was a straight "A" student; as a displaced fourth-grader in the city, my grades quite purposefully plunged to straight "Fs" – and remained there. Now, as I went out in the morning, instead of my rural paradise, I was confronted with speeding cars and freight trains. And I wandered among them with reckless abandon. One night, my friends and I, between jumping freight cars as they slowly ambled by, broke in to a storage facility on one of the tracks and removed a few small bundles of unknown content. As we hammered on them with steel rail spikes, they suddenly exploded in our faces – miraculously just burning our hands and arms rather than maiming or killing us. By my teens, I was an angry young man, purposefully doing poorly in school, purposefully running with a bad crowd, and purposefully getting into trouble on all sides – looking for a way out of this urban hell.

My chance finally came seven years into what seemed like a life sentence. When I was 15, my estranged aunt, the half-sister of my mother, invited me to work for her and her third husband for room-and-board on their newly-acquired dairy farm 80 miles north of my current home. I immediately accepted their offer – knowing full well my decision would break my mother and father's hearts. But further self-destruction was all that awaited me in the rail yard. Suddenly, from a life of zero structure and reckless abandon, I was now consumed with the responsibility of milking cows twice a day – at sunrise and sunset. Likewise, hay had to be grown and harvested; calves had to be born and fed; and manure – tons and tons of manure – had to be scraped and spread as fertilizer on the fields. Working on the dairy farm, I experienced discipline, structure and achievement for the first time in my life – and found I liked them all. My life-long leadership journey had begun!

A short time after graduating from high school, while still working on the farm, a friend of mine began writing letters to me out of the blue from a place called "The Marine Corps Recruit Depot, San Diego." In these letters, he spoke of his Drill Instructors, and his training, and the places he was going to see – all of which was tinder for a young man itching for something more than cows, manure, hay bales, and thistles. So, when he was home on leave after boot camp, I accompanied him to the recruiting office – during which time I promptly signed the paperwork. A few short weeks later I found myself at "The Marine Corps Recruit Depot San Diego" discovering a few details that my friend and the recruiter had left out of our discussions: the shaved head, the Drill Instructors screaming at you 24/7, it was quite an experience. But once the shock wore off, I knew I had found my home for the foreseeable future.

It was during these early days in my time in the Marine Corps that I met and married my wife, Alicia. We met quite by accident at a "quaint little out of the way place" more commonly referred to as a "country music dive bar" in a small city just north of San Diego. As I was surveying the landscape this particular evening, I looked across the room and immediately noticed "one of these things is not like the other" as this beautiful Latina woman stood sipping a beer among her friends. For reasons still inexplicable to me, I boldly walked across the room and asked her to dance – and much to my surprise she said "yes!" Done and done! I was smitten from that point forward. Of course, she had a long string of suitors pursuing her – which my Marine buddies and I chased off one after the other – with threats of death and bodily harm. And the rest is history as they say.

We quickly had our four children over the next six years. And that's where things got really serious. As I watched my first child being born, I was suddenly struck with the reality that I was responsible for him now and forever more – not only his mere survival and shelter – but I was also responsible for his morals, education, and life's vision. What a head trip for a 21-year-old new father who was still just a kid himself! That immense responsibility formed the background to a major decision point in my life. I knew I wanted a different outcome for my young family than I had experienced growing up. And so, I swore an oath to myself that I would do WHATEVER it took to create this new path. In short order, this secret oath was codified into three distinct goals:

1) Raise my children as a family;

2) Educate them at the world's finest universities; and

3) Provide sufficient income to buy a pair of running shoes without planning.

The first goal required me dedicating sufficient time and energy to create a safe, secure, and loving home; the second required me to chart a path that was unknown to ANYONE in my circle of family and friends. Likewise, it required me to seek formal education for myself – again and again; and the third goal, which may seem rather trivial – was truly a driving vision toward "success." For, in those early days, my young family budgeted in tens of dollars – as we knew every two weeks where EVERY ten dollars would go. As I needed a new pair of running shoes about every six months, we had to plan several weeks in advance where we would gather the required funds. And I yearned for a time when I could simply walk into a store and buy what either I or they needed.

And, in executing these three goals, *Courageous Leadership* was born within me – rather by accident and largely in hindsight. Thus, our mutual mission from this book is to create **Courageous Leadership** in you – quite purposefully – with decades of foresight.

# CHAPTER 3:
## METHODOLOGY

*Though this be madness,*
*Yet there is method in it.*
-William Shakespeare

Shakespeare had a definite method to his madness – a solid framework for each of his works that carried his audiences seamlessly from comedy to tragedy and back again. Developing your **Courageous Leadership** requires such purposeful method.

**Developmental Phases:**

It is not by accident that we measure our new leaders on their first 100 days in office, as we humans settle into patterns rather quickly and have relatively short attentions spans – to include leaders; their new administrations; and the people they lead. Thus, when enacting transformation, you should focus on achieving and solidifying significant results relatively quickly – somewhere in the vicinity of 100 days. If the transformation will take longer than 100 days, you should set intermediate milestones at no more than 100-day intervals. Thus, the construct of this book centers on a 12-week attention span (84 days) with:

- Phase 1: One week of planning & preparation;
- Phase 2: Ten weeks of Developmental Action; and
- Phase 3: One week of consolidation and future planning.

**Courageous Leadership Characteristics**

Opinions of which characteristics one could pick for development toward *Courageous Leadership* proficiency are boundless. For the purposes of this 12-week engagement, I have down-selected the infinite list to ten characteristics – which I have drawn from my own experiences and studies. Each will be methodically explained and developed in later sections. For now, I introduce them simply to incite your curiosity:

- Principled
- Technically, Cognitively, & Emotionally Aligned
- Work, Family, & Self Balanced
- Visionary
- Humble
- Powerful
- Bold
- Driven
- Charismatic
- Unreasonable

I don't expect that you will immediately understand each of these characteristics at this point – and I am sure that one or more of you are scratching your head – but for now, let's leave them be.

**Developmental Action Timing:**

Phase 2, the ten-week developmental action phase, is broken into ten 7-day sections. Each 7-day section focuses on developing one specific courageous characteristic. On the knowledge continuum, our objective is to achieve "proficiency" on each courage characteristic with the confidence and insights to pursue a lifelong path to a mastery level of knowledge.

As we are all very busy, I understand you may not be able to set aside twelve weeks in a row for developmental action. However, each 7-day section should be accomplished within its allotted 7 days. Also, you must avoid procrastinating your developmental actions beyond the allotted 7 days as you will receive the greatest developmental impact if you conduct the actions within the 7 days. And, the gaps between phases, if any, should be kept to a minimum.

Likewise, you must resist any desire to finish the developmental actions in less than twelve weeks, as your brain can only absorb so much learning within a given period of time.

**Development Tools:**
Like the Courageous Leadership Characteristics above, opinions of which development tools one could select for achievement of Courageous Leadership Proficiency are unlimited. And again, certainly, as one strives for Courageous Leadership Mastery, you would need to expand the list. For the purposes of this developmental engagement, I have refined the unlimited list to the below five tools:
1. Journaling
2. Semi-Structured Conversations
3. Mentor A.I.R. Hot Washes
4. Individual Mission Statement
5. Individual Development Plan

**Journal**

As a matter of personal and professional development, *courageous leaders* should journal daily for somewhere between 15 and 30 minutes. In a quiet setting, this time includes contemplating the day's events and then capturing them in writing. Captured thoughts should, among other topics, span the continuum of the ten courage characteristics. During these twelve weeks, you will journal for approximately 10 hours with the intent that doing so will become a life-long practice. As you journal, take particular care to capture the emotions, surprises, and new insights you experience and gain. You can find a template for Journaling at www.FlatterLeadership.com/Journal

**Semi-Structured Conversations:**

Semi-structured conversations are a means of gathering information through focused discussions. Prior to the conversation, the data collector writes out a few questions to help guide the dialogue while not overly-restricting the potential scope of the discussion. Throughout the different developmental sections of this developmental journey, you will conduct 28 such conversations. You can find a template for these conversations at www.FlatterLeadership.com/SSC

**Mentor A.I.R. Hot Washes**

During the twelve weeks, you will add several people to your network of personal and professional associates. Likewise, you currently have in your life friends and family. One or more of these people should be invited to participate in your transformational journey as a Mentor. As you conduct developmental actions – such as journaling, drafting Individual Mission Statements, or conducting Semi-Structured Conversations – you should discuss these activities in real time with your Mentor. These discussions are called *A.I.R. Hot Washes* – in that you will seek Advice, Information, and Referrals from your Mentor on the particular subjects. You can find a template for these Hot Washes at www.FlatterLeadership.com/AIR

**Individual Mission Statement (IMS)**

An Individual Mission Statement (IMS) is a document that collects and communicates information regarding what you intend to do with your life – i.e. *"What is your Life's Mission?"*. This document is going to serve as the guiding text upon which you choose to live your life from this point forward. Don't over-complicate it – but, at the same time, write it with the magnitude of importance it deserves. You will update your IMS regularly as your life changes and your principles mature – so it is not set in stone either. However, its foundations should remain solid while your changes are largely tweaks that adjust to emerging circumstances. You can find a template for this document at www.FlatterLeadership.com/IMS

**Individual Development Plan (IDP)**

An Individual Development Plan (IDP) is a document that collects and communicates the developmental actions needed to close the gaps between your current level of knowledge and required level of knowledge. It is usually phased at appropriate intervals to capture near, mid, and far-term developmental requirements. Likewise, as it transitions fuzzy goals into finite objectives, the IDP contains clear milestones that identify developmental completion points. You can find a template for this document at www.FlatterLeadership.com/IDP

**Developmental Actions:**

These twelve weeks purposefully ask a lot from you – for transformational leadership development is by its very nature – hard work. And I recognize each of us learns differently. But I nonetheless challenge you to complete this formidable body of work. When you are finished you will have completed:

- 12 weeks of Journaling
- 28 Semi-Structured Conversations
- 12 Mentor/Protégé A.I.R. Hot Washes
- 1 Draft Individual Mission Statement (IMS)
- 11 IMS Reviews
- 1 Draft Individual Development Plan (IDP)
- 12 IDP Reviews
- 1 Draft Lifetime Goals & Objectives (LG&O)
- 1 Revised LG&O
- 16 New or Strengthened Relationships
- 1 T•C•E Alignment

- 10 T•C•E Alignment Reviews
- 1 W•F•S Balance
- 9 W•F•S Balance Reviews
- 12 Courageous Leadership Characteristics Measurements
- 10 Courageous Leadership Characteristics Gap Analyses

**Outcomes:**

During these twelve weeks, through completing these developmental actions, you will achieve a level of "proficiency" with each of the ten *Courageous Leadership* characteristics – which will in turn serve as a baseline for your further leadership development.

Concurrently, and perhaps even more importantly, you will either draft for the first time or further clarify and then begin executing your lifetime goals & objectives. This second outcome is especially critical in that it provides the tangible products upon which you will leverage your new-found leadership abilities.

## Day-Zero Measuring:

To measure your progress toward your goal of *Courageous Leadership* Proficiency, we must first measure where you start at "Day-Zero." We will then measure your levels of knowledge at the end of each 7-day section and again at the end of the twelve weeks. With those objectives in mind, please complete the below matrix to measure your day-zero level of knowledge of the ten *Courageous Leadership* Characteristics. Keep in mind, there is no value in exaggerating your level of knowledge regarding the characteristics. You can find a template of this document at www.FlatterLeadership.com/Assessment

For each characteristic below, select the descriptor score that best matches your current knowledge level

| CHARACTERISTIC | SCORE 0-10 |
|---|---|
| Principled | |
| TCE | |
| WFS | |
| Vision | |
| Humility | |
| Powerful | |
| Bold | |
| Driven | |
| Charismatic | |
| Unreasonable | |
| Total Score: | |

| SCORE | DESCRIPTORS |
|---|---|
| 0 | You are unaware of this characteristic as a value-added part of leadership |
| 1 | You have just learned about this characteristic |
| 2 | You know about this characteristic but do not yet understand its value to your leadership |
| 3 | You understand the value of this characteristic but are not yet prepared to purposefully exhibit it |
| 4 | You understand the value of this characteristic and uneasily try to exhibit it when you remember |
| 5 | You understand the value of this characteristic and comfortably exhibit it when you remember |
| 6 | You comfortably exhibit this characteristic on almost all occasions |
| 7 | You recognize the growth of this characteristic in yourself and are naturally and confidently exhibiting it as a central part of your leadership |
| 8 | You are recognized by others for this characteristic as a particular strength |
| 9 | You comfortably mentor others in exhbiting this characteristic |
| 10 | You are the ideal example of this characteristic |

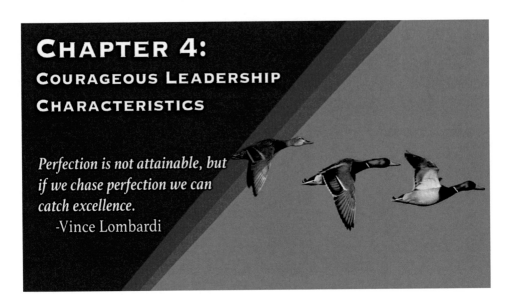

# CHAPTER 4:

## COURAGEOUS LEADERSHIP
## CHARACTERISTICS

*Perfection is not attainable, but if we chase perfection we can catch excellence.*
   -Vince Lombardi

Much like Lombardi's unattainable quest for perfection on the football field, our life-long pursuit of Courageous Leadership Mastery is equally unattainable – yet nonetheless a noble and worthy ideal. As we identify, discuss, and develop within ourselves the ten Courageous Leadership Characteristics in the next several sections, we must never lose sight of that fact.

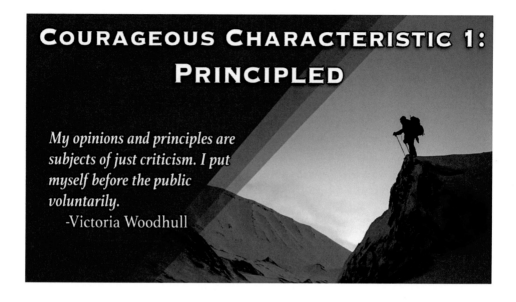

# COURAGEOUS CHARACTERISTIC 1: PRINCIPLED

*My opinions and principles are subjects of just criticism. I put myself before the public voluntarily.*
-Victoria Woodhull

### *I am a Courageous Leader… therefore, I am Principled!*

With courage as the foundation upon which leadership stands, principles are the pillars upon which courageous leaders conduct their lives. As courageous leaders, we must identify and communicate our principles "before the public" as Woodhull did in her life-long fight to gain voting privileges for women in the United States. By definition, a "principle" is:

*"a fundamental truth or proposition that serves as the foundation for a system of belief and behavior..."*

The principles of courageous leadership are the ***Courageous Leadership Characteristics***. Being *"principled"* is not only the first courageous characteristic but it is also the foundational characteristic – for, in order to be principled, one must first subscribe to the ideal that they will live a principled life! Concurrently, in order to subscribe to the other courageous leadership characteristics, one must first subscribe to the ideal that they will live the characteristics within a principled life.

Principles are closely associates with morals – which are defined as:

*"a person's own standards of behavior or beliefs concerning what is and is not acceptable for them to do."*

With that definition, morals are the principles you personally choose upon which you bound and perform your conduct. Principles simultaneously *require* you exhibit certain behaviors while *preventing* you from exhibiting other behaviors.

Leaders must make decisions almost always without complete information. Their guiding principles are what fill in the white spaces to consistently inform the leader about what is right and wrong.

You validate your adherence to these principles through the principled execution of your life, for principles can only be sufficiently communicated through action. Attempting to describe them in either written or verbal proclamations rings hollow and appears braggadocios. In the case of principles, they must be communicated through your actions – i.e. walking the walk versus talking the talk. Likewise, they can only be attributed to you by others through their recognition of your consistently demonstrated actions.

Thus, when you are first identifying your principles, you must identify what morals you are demonstrating through your actions. Likewise, when you are developing the courageous characteristics, you can only measure your progress through the increased demonstration of each.

Long ago, I subscribed to the guiding principle of dedicating my working life to serve as my children's transformational generation – thereby lifting our family from generation-after-generation of day-laborers to one of college-educated, skilled, white-collar professionals. You can argue the merits of this principle, but it nonetheless served as my guiding beacon for over 30 years. Today, I take pride in the fact that not only have I transformed my personal fortunes, but my children attended and graduated from the world's finest universities and each has a successful career, owns their own home, and is happily married (so far, so good...).

Of course, there are several associated principles that one must also subscribe to in order to fulfill this guiding principle – such as dedicating sufficient time and attention to achieve the guiding principle; and a personal dedication to life-long learning – most notably for me – accumulating advanced formal education degrees.

When I was a newly commissioned Lieutenant, one of my Marines was arrested for possession of anabolic steroids – which are a controlled substance under military law. This particular Marine had just returned from combat where he had been decorated for his bravery.

At that time, the Marine Corps had a "Zero Tolerance" policy for drug possession and use. However, using my self-defined principles, I differentiated between a Marine taking mind-altering drugs and a young, skinny kid using steroids in an attempt to bulk up. Of course, it was foolish of him to assume the health risks associated with steroid use, but in his mind, he simply wanted to become stronger – and therefore become a better Marine. And, of course, he knew the steroids were illegal and he needed to be punished for his purposefully illegal activities. But in this instance, if he were discharged for the drug use and possession, he would lose all his Veteran benefits and be required to forfeit his medals. In my assessment, again using my principles, I thought such punishment would be far too severe for the infractions for which he was guilty. Thus, I fought to retain him in the Marine Corps – against the wishes of my superior – who thought he deserved the maximum punishment.

I am not telling this story as criticism of his principles, for he was entitled to his as you and I are entitled to ours. Rather, I tell the story partly as a clear demonstration of genuinely conflicting principles. Neither of us was clearly "right" nor were we "wrong." We were simply acting upon our deeply held principles. And I would expect that he firmly stands for his principles as I expect myself to firmly stand for mine.

In the end, a review board voted to retain the young Marine in the Corps – and he again distinguished himself in combat just a few months later – and then left the Corps for a successful career in Law Enforcement. Whew!

## Socrates

Socrates was a Greek philosopher who lived from 470 to 399 B.C. He is credited as the founder of Western Philosophy and, thus, informed much of the way we think about ourselves and our world. Socrates' style of inquiry – known as the *Socratic Method* – is a process of investigation that literally questions – with question after question after question – with each new question requiring the answerer to delve deeper and deeper into their reasoning. As you might imagine, this aggressive style of dialogue might be frustrating with any subject, let alone, when it is used to question the legitimacy of the ruling government.

But such was Socrates' style and subject. And it got him in deep trouble with the Athenian Government – reaching an apex in 399 B.C. For, Athens at the time was in a state of unrest. It had been defeated by Sparta in the Peloponnesian War (431–404 BC) and needed to regain stability and reestablish the confidence and alliance of its citizenry. But in comes Socrates and his questions! Socrates' lectures – known as dialogues – were primarily on the subjects of virtue and ethics – which Athenian leaders considered purposeful subversions of the State's authority to rule.

Ultimately, Socrates was officially accused of two crimes: First for "refusing to respect and worship the gods officially recognized by the State" – as his questioning was not viewed as a method to reveal more truth about the gods, but as a lack of belief or even as an introduction of new gods. And secondly, he was accused of "corrupting the youth." Both crimes were punishable by death should he be convicted of either.

At his trail, in his usual provocative style, rather than deferring to the jury's authority, Socrates agitated the 500 members by claiming to be the wisest person in the room because he was the only one among them who would admit their absolute ignorance of all things. Not surprisingly, Socrates' trial ended in a conviction and he was sentenced to death by drinking poison hemlock.

After his conviction, Socrates had the opportunity to escape as his disciples were prepared to bribe the prison guards, but Socrates accepted the sentence. His rationale – and thus the ultimate subscription to his principles – was that if he were to escape, his life would have been meaningless, for he had dedicated his life to living and teaching the Principle of Civil Obedience.

# Principled Developmental Action

**Developmental Purpose:**

The purpose of this seven-day *Principled-Development Action Phase* is to:

- Better understand the need to be principled;
- Verbalize and capture the principles that are important to you;
- Translate those principles into an Individual Mission Statement (IMS);
- Measure your current level of core principles;
- Compare the findings to your IMS; and
- Identify and take courageous action to close the gaps.

**Journaling**

During these seven days, focus your journaling on your principles. Likewise, journal about the principles of the people with which you will have semi-structured conversations. As you journal, take particular care to capture the emotions, surprises, and new insights you experience and gain. As you begin consciously living the principles you have drafted, journal your observed actions executing those principles.

In your journal, verbally identify the differences between your observed principles and desired principles so that you may begin closing the gaps.

**Draft your *Individual Mission Statement (IMS):***

Per the example below, draft your Individual Mission Statement (IMS) as a simple document that collects and communicates information regarding what you intend to do with your life. This document is going to serve as the guiding text upon which you choose to live your life from this point forward. Don't over-complicate it – but, at the same time, write it with the magnitude of importance it deserves. You will update your IMS regularly as your life changes and your principles mature – so it is not set in stone either. However, its foundations should remain solid while your changes are largely tweaks that adjust to emerging circumstances. Likewise, we will use this IMS later as a basis in identifying your life's goals & objectives.

## Sample Individual Mission Statement

| | |
|---|---|
| **Who am I?**<br>• I am a loving Spouse, Parent, Sibling, Friend, & Leader. | **In these roles, I am guided by:**<br>• My love for my Wife, Family, and Fellow Man;<br>• My commitment to continually educating myself and others; and<br>• My services as a Courageous Leader. |
| **What do I believe in?**<br>• The *Courageous Characteristics*<br>  • Principled<br>  • TCE Aligned<br>  • WFS Balanced<br>  • Visionary<br>  • Humble<br>  • Powerful<br>  • Bold<br>  • Driven<br>  • Charismatic<br>  • Unreasonable | **How do these beliefs guide my life?**<br>• I subscribe to the *Courageous Characteristics* to guide my life as I fulfill my leadership roles. |
| **What are my deepest passions?**<br>• I have a passion for leading and developing leaders. | **How do these passions impact my life?**<br>• My role as a father is primarily that of leader and leader developer;<br>• My role as a businessman is primarily that of leader and leader developer; and<br>• My role as a community servant is primarily that of leader and leader developer. |
| **What do I aspire to be?**<br>• I aspire to leave behind a vibrant company | **How do these aspirations influence my actions?**<br>• So that my family and team may continue to fulfill their life's goals & objectives. |

**Semi-Structured Conversations:**

To help you further articulate your principles, arrange and conduct semi-structured conversations with:

- Yourself,
- Your significant other, and
- A leader you consider especially principled (preferably not your Mentor).

Prior to the conversations, observe your subjects and document in your journal the principles you see in their day-to-day actions.

At the beginning of the conversations, summarize the philosophy of *Courageous Leadership* and the courageous characteristic of being principled from your own understanding for the interviewee.

During the conversations, capture the findings in your journal. As you journal, please take particular care to capture the emotions, surprises, and new insights you experience and gain. Questions for these conversations might include:

- What principles do they see you exhibiting?
- What principles do they personally subscribe to?
- What principles do you and they feel are important to your family and/or organization?
- What were the principles of the best person they have worked for?
- What were the principles of the worst person they have worked for?

In your journal, verbally identify the differences between your observed principles and desired principles so that you may begin closing the gaps.

**A.I.R. Hot Wash:**

Schedule a conversation with your Mentor to discuss:

- **Advice**: What advice does he/she have for you regarding principles in general – and specifically your level of principles.
- **Information**: Ask your Mentor for sources of additional information that they have found useful regarding principles.

- **Referrals**: Ask who you should speak to further about principles.
  - In your journal, verbally identify the differences between your observed principles and desired principles so that you may begin closing the gaps.

**Culminating Actions:**

Given the identified gap between your current principles and desired principles:

- Include *Principled Development* in your IDP. Identify developmental goals and activities. Developmental activities may include training (classroom, on-line, webinar), mentoring (either being a mentor or protégé), college courses, books (including audiobooks), developmental projects, stretch assignments, job shadowing, job rotation, networking opportunities, conferences, etc.
- Review and, if needed, modify your draft IMS to match your current understanding of principles.
- Adjust your life and calendar accordingly to achieve your desired principles so that you may fulfill your IMS.

**7-Day Summary:**
During this seven-day *Principled-Development Action Phase*, you have:

- Conducted in-depth self-reflection;
- Held semi-structured conversations with significant people in your personal and professional lives;
- Sought advice, information, & referrals from your Mentor;
- Captured your emotions, surprises, and new insights from these 7 days of development in your journal;
- Added *Principles Development* to your IDP;
- Drafted an Individual Mission Statement (IMS); and
- Began living your IMS.

**Bottom Line Value Creation:**

- Now that you have captured your Courageous Principles in an Individual Mission Statement, you have a guidepost upon which you can not only direct your personal and professional lives, but also use to guide the remainder of your 12-Week Development.

For each characteristic below, select the descriptor score that best matches your current knowledge level

| CHARACTERISTIC | SCORE 0-10 |
|---|---|
| Principled | |
| TCE | |
| WFS | |
| Vision | |
| Humility | |
| Powerful | |
| Bold | |
| Driven | |
| Charismatic | |
| Unreasonable | |
| Total Score: | |

| SCORE | DESCRIPTORS |
|---|---|
| 0 | You are unaware of this characteristic as a value-added part of leadership |
| 1 | You have just learned about this characteristic |
| 2 | You know about this characteristic but do not yet understand its value to your leadership |
| 3 | You understand the value of this characteristic but are not yet prepared to purposefully exhibit it |
| 4 | You understand the value of this characteristic and uneasily try to exhibit it when you remember |
| 5 | You understand the value of this characteristic and comfortably exhibit it when you remember |
| 6 | You comfortably exhibit this characteristic on almost all occasions |
| 7 | You recognize the growth of this characteristic in yourself and are naturally and confidently exhibiting it as a central part of your leadership |
| 8 | You are recognized by others for this characteristic as a particular strength |
| 9 | You comfortably mentor others in exhbiting this characteristic |
| 10 | You are the ideal example of this characteristic |

Now that you have completed your seven days of *Principles* development, let's take a snapshot of your knowledge level. After you measure your current level of knowledge per the matrix above, look back at your Day-Zero level of *Principles* knowledge. We would expect that your level has increased due to your developmental actions.

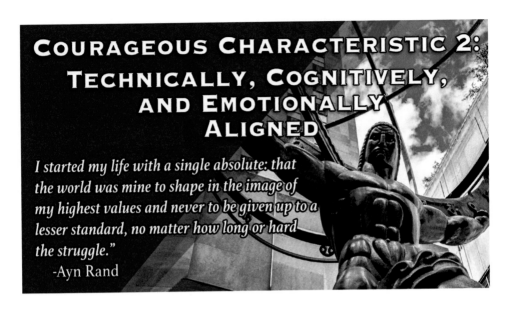

# COURAGEOUS CHARACTERISTIC 2: TECHNICALLY, COGNITIVELY, AND EMOTIONALLY ALIGNED

*I started my life with a single absolute: that the world was mine to shape in the image of my highest values and never to be given up to a lesser standard, no matter how long or hard the struggle."*
-Ayn Rand

## *I am a Courageous Leader… therefore, I am T•C•E Aligned!*

Per Rand's suggestion, as we perform our leadership activities, we should appropriately shape our world using three broad categories of intelligence: 1) Technical, 2) Cognitive, and 3) Emotional.

Technical intelligence is the collection of knowledge, skills, and abilities needed to function within your chosen profession. Technical actions are largely transactional in that you engage in a specific activity to produce a specific output. There is usually one way to perform the action to achieve the result. Once the transaction is completed, you then move on to another activity to produce another output. Likewise, technical activities are largely linear – in that you progress in a straight line from pre-determined action to anticipated product.

Cognitive intelligence is your ability to problem solve through gathering data, conducting analysis, making decisions, and then writing execution plans. As there are likely established decision-making protocols and accepted research methods within your organization, cognitive intelligence is largely transactional. Cognitive intelligence is used principally for determining how to best manage *things* – such as raw materials, office space, or time – in an ongoing effort to minimize costs while maximizing value outputs.

And finally, emotional intelligence is your willingness & ability to create and strengthen relationships with *people* to gain and increase their enthusiasm to support and achieve your goals & objectives. As each person is different, with varied personalities and preferences, the methods of emotionally engaging them are equally varied – limited only by your willingness & abilities. Emotional intelligence is very transformational as it forever changes the relationships and mutual actions between participants moving forward – toward the purpose of creating value beyond that which was possible beforehand.

The below chart contains some simple examples of the different types of actions related to the differing uses of intelligence:

| Profession | Technical Actions | Cognitive Actions | Emotional Actions |
|---|---|---|---|
| Marine | Shooting, Moving, & Communicating | Identifying how many Recruits should be hired this year | Visiting deployed forces on Christmas Day |
| Mechanic | Turning the wrench left to loosen and right to tighten | Determining whether to rebuild or replace an old engine | Chatting with your customers to put them at ease with your diagnosis and estimate |
| Medical Doctor | Learning an adult has 206 bones | Deciding on a splint or a cast | Discussing options with the family |
| Lawyer | Learning the Law | Selecting the best precedence to support your legal strategy | Writing a compelling closing argument |
| Civil Engineer | Learning physics, mathematics, project management, and design | Balancing cost, risk, and schedule | Deciding to hire an experienced engineer because he will mesh well with your existing team |
| Computer Scientist | Coding | Requirements Development | Delivering a convincing brief to the C-Suite |

| | | | |
|---|---|---|---|
| **Physicist** | E=MC2 | Experimenting with the speed of light to determine why it is constant | Wearing an eccentric hairstyle |
| **Police Officer** | Learning the Penal Code | Deciding to give a verbal warning instead of a ticket | Building rapport with the residents of your city |
| **Auto Manufacturer** | Cataloguing the part numbers for each vehicle in your inventory | Selecting a competitive mix of vehicle styles | Successfully rallying your factory to reach a quarterly goal |
| **Steak House Owner** | Selecting good cuts of meat at the butcher | Making menu choices | Selling the sizzle! |

In the early days of our careers, our "value" to ourselves, others, and our organizations is largely technical. How fast can we re-build an engine; how well can we recite the law; and can we dig a hole to the exact specifications in our instructions. "Work" using technical intelligence is often physically and/or psychologically exhausting. It provides a measure of achievement related to the level of exhaustion. Likewise, technical achievement can be directly measured and admired as outcomes, such as a repaired engine, compiled precedence citations, or a deep hole.

As we get promoted to management positions or otherwise find ourselves in advanced roles, we contribute more cognitively. Should I re-build or replace the engine; do I have enough evidence to convict; should I dig a hole or drive a pile? "Work" using cognitive intelligence is usually not physically exhausting but can be quite mentally exhausting. It therefore also provides a level of achievement correlated to the level of effort. Likewise, cognitive achievement can be directly measured and admired through tangible products such as written plans.

As we advance to leadership positions, our greatest value lies mostly in emotional intelligence activities. Look at the "Emotional Actions" column in the chart above. "Work" using emotional intelligence is largely void of technical labor. And it is largely void of the reward of physical exhaustion to measure our "work." Thus, it does not usually provide the tangible feedback of physical products. As such, when you are asked at the end of a long, busy day "What did you do today?" it can be difficult to explain in a sentence or two – or point to some evidence that you "worked" hard from morning to night. But, regardless of direct evidence or tangible products, emotional intelligence is where you can produce the greatest value and it is where you should spend the greatest amount of your time "working." But it is emotional intelligence that propels people, teams, and organizations beyond simply surviving into excelling. A coach's speech at halftime to rally his team; a doctor who congratulates you for lowering your cholesterol; or an executive leader who knows your name and thanks you in front of your peers for doing a great job.

One of the greatest challenges of using emotional intelligence is that you must willfully choose to perform less technical and cognitive "work" so that you have sufficient time to dedicate to your more important emotional "work." And, as all skills atrophy without regular use, I am purposefully asking you to no longer strive to be the best mechanic in the shop; the most efficient coder in the lab; or the fastest runner in the platoon. Rather, I am asking you to become the best leader you can be by leaving those titles to others on your teams. They need and deserve your Courageous Leadership. Thus, as courageous leaders it is our responsibility to ensure we *align* our actions to the appropriate type of intelligence that is needed in each situation. Further, it is our responsibility to ensure our people and organizations are aligned to their appropriate type of intelligence at any given level and at any given time.

Generally, there is a migration from T→C→E actions as we progress in our lives and careers – but, ultimately that maturation is as varied as are people – with no right or wrong path. The movement from one to another – or lack thereof – is a product of both willingness & ability. Likewise, regardless of position, there are times – hours, days, and even years – when it is appropriate for each of us to be aligned in one or the other. However, my primary point is that if you are willing then you are likely able – but you must first understand and then strive toward the ideal that your T•C•E Alignment should lean heavily toward emotional.

    Within months after finishing my education in "Multi-Variate Regression Analysis," I was assigned to a two-person Think Tank to assist in reinventing the processes through which the Marine Corps conducted human resources development. Ironically, my partner in this effort was a professional artist who draws and paints everything from landscape to portrait from life. We could not have been more different in our technical, cognitive, and emotional alignments. For I viewed and acted on the world through logic and quantitative analysis, while he viewed and acted on the world through color and light! You can only imagine the spirited debates that occurred as we were sequestered away for weeks on end – just the two of us and our research materials. However, once we got through this "storming" phase of our teaming effort, we began to recognize and appreciate the brilliance of the General who had selected and assigned us to this project – for, through her technical, cognitive, and emotional alignment – she saw the value of bringing our two different word views together to achieve some very complex and challenging goals. In the end, the time I spent on that Think Tank were two of the most broadening and enlightening years of my leadership journey. Thank you, Sir! Thank you, Ma'am!

# Indra Nooyi

1

Indra Nooyi, who became the CEO and president of PepsiCo in 2006, is a strong example of a T•C•E-Aligned leader.

Nooyi's resume checks all the appropriate boxes for an extraordinary performer and world class success. She received bachelor's degrees in Physics, Chemistry and Mathematics from Madras Christian College of the University of Madras in 1974; an MBA from Indian Institute of Management Calcutta in 1976; and a Master's Degree in Public and Private Management at Yale School of Management in 1980. She has held management positions at Johnson & Johnson, the textile firm Mettur Beardsell, Boston Consulting Group; and strategy position at Sea Brown Boveri and Motorola.

But what makes Nooyi exceptional among the exceptional, is her mastery of her T•C•E alignment and her concurrent ability to use that alignment to create a culture of emotional intelligence within both PepsiCo's business strategy and its employees' everyday performance. With the proof in the pudding as her efforts produce both profitability and stability for the long term, as PepsiCo stock

[1] By World Economic Forum - originally posted to Flickr as Indra Nooyi - World Economic Forum Annual Meeting Davos 2008, CC BY-SA 2.0, https://commons.wikimedia.org/w/index.php?curid=4486071

has risen quickly during her tenure, closing in on that of rival Coca-Cola, and the company's annual net profit has risen from $2.7 billion to $6.5 billion.

As a supporting example of her T•C•E alignment, Nooyi is famous for personally writing letters – over four hundred a year - to the *parents* of PepsiCo senior executives. She explains her rationale for this practice in stating that when she returned to India as a successful adult, family members and neighbors who visited her family home congratulated her mother on Nooyi's success, hardly speaking with Nooyi at all. She soon realized that parents, who are largely responsible for their children's success, rarely receive their due acknowledgement. Thus, the emotionally intelligent 400+ letters per year! If she has the time for such T•C•E alignment in pursuit of her insatiable requirements, we can certainly strive to demonstrate the same!

# T•C•E Developmental Action

**Developmental Purpose:**

The purpose of this seven-day *T•C•E-Development Action Phase* is to:

- Explore your current T•C•E Alignment percentages;
- Identify where your T•C•E Alignment percentages should be; and
- Take action to achieve your optimal T•C•E Alignment.

**Journal:**

Journal these 7 days with a focus on your T•C•E Alignment actions across your daily activities.

The first day of this developmental period, stop and capture your T•C•E Alignment actions for each previous hour. As you journal, label your activities as T, C, or E. Also, as you journal, please take particular care to capture the emotions, surprises, and new insights you experience and gain. After one full day, tally your T•C•E activities. Then analyze the results to determine your current ratio of activities. Plot your alignment percentages in the table below:

| Current T•C•E Alignment | | |
|---|---|---|
| **Technical** | **Cognitive** | **Emotional** |
| % | % | % |

**Semi-Structured Conversations:**

To assist in identifying your appropriate T•C•E Alignment for this period of your life and career, hold semi-structured conversations with:

- Yourself,
- Your significant other, and
- A leader you consider especially T•C•E Aligned (preferably not your Mentor).

Prior to the conversations, observe your subjects and document in your journal the T•C•E Alignment you see in their day-to-day actions.

At the beginning of the conversations, summarize the philosophy of Courageous Leadership and the T•C•E Alignment of the interviewee.

During the conversations, capture the findings in your journal. As you journal, please take particular care to capture the emotions, surprises, and new insights you experience and gain. Questions for these conversations might include:

- How important is achieving T•C•E Alignment?
- What is the appropriate T•C•E Alignment for me at this stage in my life and career?
- As a leader, how do you know if you are spending the right amount of time in each of the categories (T•C•E)?
- What has been helpful to you in making changes (i.e., increasing time spent developing relationships)?

In your journal, verbally identify the differences between your observed T•C•E Alignment and desired T•C•E Alignment so that you may begin closing the gaps.

**A.I.R. Hot Wash:**
Schedule a conversation with your Mentor to discuss:

- **Advice**: What advice does he/she have for you regarding T•C•E Alignment in general – and specifically your level of T•C•E Alignment.
- **Information**: Ask your Mentor for sources of additional information that they have found useful regarding T•C•E Alignment.
- **Referrals**: Ask who should you speak to further about T•C•E Alignment.

In your journal, verbally identify the differences between your observed T•C•E Alignment and desired T•C•E Alignment so that you may begin closing the gaps.

With your identified T•C•E Alignment and the conversations accomplished, identify your appropriate T•C•E Alignment in the table below.

| Appropriate T•C•E Alignment | | |
|---|---|---|
| **Technical** | **Cognitive** | **Emotional** |
| % | % | % |

**T•C•E Culminating Actions**: Given the identified gap between your current T•C•E Alignment and desired T•C•E Alignment:
- Include *T•C•E Alignment* in your IDP. Identify developmental goals and activities. Developmental activities may include training (classroom, on-line, webinar), mentoring (either being a mentor or protégé), college courses, books (including audiobooks), developmental projects, stretch assignments, job shadowing, job rotation, networking opportunities, conferences, etc.
- Review and, if needed, modify your draft IMS to match your current understanding of T•C•E Alignment.
- Adjust your life and calendar accordingly to achieve your desired T•C•E Alignment so that you may fulfill your IMS.

**7-Day Summary:**
During this seven-day *T•C•E Alignment Development Action Phase*, you have:
- Conducted in-depth self-reflection;
- Held semi-structured conversations with significant people in your personal and professional lives;
- Sought advice, information, & referrals from your Mentor;
- Captured your emotions, surprises, and new insights from these 7 days of development in your journal;
- Identified the appropriate T•C•E Alignment for this time in your life;
- Identified actions to successfully implement your T•C•E Alignment;
- Added *T•C•E Alignment* to your IDP; and

- Took the initial steps to adjust your life and calendar to meet your T•C•E Alignment.

**Bottom Line Value Creation:**
- With your correct T•C•E Alignment identified at this point in your life and career, you now have a focused view of how to maximize your personal value delivery to yourself, your family, your team, and your organizations.

For each characteristic below, select the descriptor score that best matches your current knowledge level

| Characteristic | Score 0-10 |
|---|---|
| **Principled** | |
| **TCE** | |
| **WFS** | |
| **Vision** | |
| **Humility** | |
| **Powerful** | |
| **Bold** | |
| **Driven** | |
| **Charismatic** | |
| **Unreasonable** | |
| **Total Score:** | |

| Score | Descriptors |
|---|---|
| 0 | You are unaware of this characteristic as a value-added part of leadership |
| 1 | You have just learned about this characteristic |
| 2 | You know about this characteristic but do not yet understand its value to your leadership |
| 3 | You understand the value of this characteristic but are not yet prepared to purposefully exhibit it |
| 4 | You understand the value of this characteristic and uneasily try to exhibit it when you remember |
| 5 | You understand the value of this characteristic and comfortably exhibit it when you remember |
| 6 | You comfortably exhibit this characteristic on almost all occasions |
| 7 | You recognize the growth of this characteristic in yourself and are naturally and confidently exhibiting it as a central part of your leadership |
| 8 | You are recognized by others for this characteristic as a particular strength |
| 9 | You comfortably mentor others in exhbiting this characteristic |
| 10 | You are the ideal example of this characteristic |

Now that you have completed your seven days of *T•C•E Alignment* development, let's take a snapshot of your knowledge level. After you assess your current level of knowledge per the matrix above, look back at your Day-Zero level of *T•C•E alignment* knowledge. We would expect that your level has increased due to your developmental actions.

49

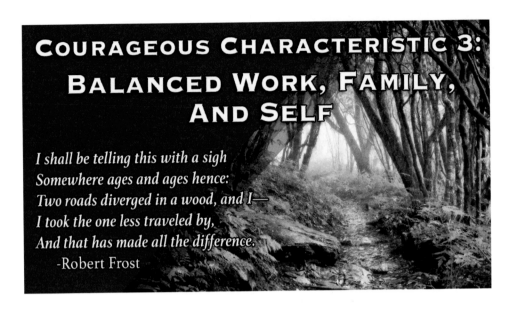

# COURAGEOUS CHARACTERISTIC 3:
# BALANCED WORK, FAMILY, AND SELF

*I shall be telling this with a sigh*
*Somewhere ages and ages hence:*
*Two roads diverged in a wood, and I—*
*I took the one less traveled by,*
*And that has made all the difference.*
-Robert Frost

***I am a Courageous Leader… therefore, I strive for***
**W•F•S Balance*!***

W.F.s

w.F.s

w•f•S

W•F•S

Courageous leaders take the road less-travelled.

I must confess striving for this balance is my hardest struggle as a *courageous leader*. As I wrote of earlier, when my first child was born, and as I looked into his newborn face, I swore a secret oath to myself that I would do WHATEVER it took to provide a better life for this tiny, purple baby. As you can quickly surmise, such a promise required significant work on my behalf to achieve. Yet, I was also able to surmise, relatively quickly, that raising my children as a family was not achievable if I ignored them in the process. Concurrently, working myself to death to educate four children who would not know who I was did not spell "success" either. So, my wife and I purposefully created a W•F•S Balance that provided both the needed work hours and the family time.

Like many ideals, W•F•S Balance is an objective worthy of pursuit, but most often actually achieved in short glimpses. The gigantic W seems ever-present, sucking all-available oxygen from our other life priorities. We yearn for more F time, but often feel compelled to W, W, W to provide for our families. And the tiny S seems mostly ignored. However, those demonstrated facts do not absolve us from displaying the needed courage every minute of every day to achieve the appropriate W•F•S Balance.

No one category of W•F•S should be absolute, nor should any be non-existent. In the short term, one category may legitimately push aside the other two. But you must have the courage to evaluate on a regular basis if the short-term necessity still exists and not procrastinate getting back in balance. Life is a journey – not a destination. Thus, you must consciously avoid using "necessity" as an excuse to work for a lack of investment in family and self. For if you get to the "finish line" alone – you have not won! The relative size of the hours committed does not necessarily reflect the actual size of the priority. Almost without fail, if you are going to achieve break-out success in life, then you are going to have to work long hours, but not to the point of absolutely ignoring family and self.

Of course, W•F•S Balance legitimately modulates over time as requirements dictate. There will be periods of time when even the most disciplined courageous leader cannot control their commitments. In the early part of your career, when you are laying the foundation upon which the remainder of your life's hopes and dreams will stand, you should expect to have a gigantic W – but again – not at the absolute detriment of either family or self. And focusing on "self" is not selfish – even when you have a house full of little ones who possess legitimate, insatiable needs. For you are their "Golden Goose" and if you are not able to function – either due to exhaustion or illness or worse – then they do not have what they need.

One simple tool I use to achieve W•F•S Balance is to color-code my calendar – with a different color for each type of activity. Work at my HQ is dark blue; work in the city is purple; work on travel is orange; community service is silver; Doctor's appointments are pink; exercise is red; family activities are dark green; friend activities are light green; and so on and so forth. With this method, I can glance at my calendar to see my week-by-week or monthly balance.

As a real-world example of my personal struggles with W•F•S Balance, I offer an epiphany from my early career. It's no secret that military families move around a lot. My family and I were no exception to that reality as we moved eleven times during our twenty-two years of service. In addition to these frequent moves, the military requires "up or out" as you must either get promoted or seek a career elsewhere. As such, you are continually seeking plumb assignments that would keep you competitive for promotion while unpacking boxes from your most-recent move.

In my case, the first of these plumb assignments and moves after we were married and had our first child was as a Drill Instructor in San Diego – which is a seven-days-a-week; 18-20 hours a day job; with at least one of every three nights spent sleeping at work. Regularly, during this time, I told my wife – "After this is done, things will slow down a bit…"

Next was a year-long college preparatory school that, due to the academic pace, required me to move out of our home and into the school house – just to survive. Again, I told her regularly – "After this is done, things will slow down a bit…"

Then on to college in Seattle with the same priorities and promises – "After this is done, things will slow down a bit…"

And then on to the Basic School in Virginia – but this is where the W•F•S epiphany hit me – we had moved three times in six years – and each time for an ever-increasing level of required work commitment on my behalf – and during a time in which I had largely ignored my wife and growing family.

How many times would I make the same unfulfilled promise of "slowing down?" Something had to change! And that "something" was me! From that day forward, I took great care to sleep on my own pillow as often as physically possible; move into our new homes – to include hanging pictures, emptying boxes, and installing curtains – within the same week as accepting occupancy; and arriving home for dinner at our table at 6:00 pm as the rule rather than the exception.

# Margaret Thatcher

2

It might initially seem odd to include someone whose nickname was the "*Iron Lady*" in a story about W•F•S Balance – but such was the life of Margaret Thatcher – as she balanced her steely determination on the world stage with a 52-year marriage and motherhood of twins.

Thatcher, who was unquestionably one of the most formidable political influences of the 20th century, came from modest beginnings as the daughter of a grocer. Born in pre-World War II Britain, her world was divided across strict class lines. Although a few women were gaining their places in the workforce, the majority were expected to stay at home and raise families. But Margaret chose *the path less taken* and pursued work through a career in politics. She was quickly identified by the Tory (conservative) Party as a future political star and was being urged by many to continue her career.

But then came her marriage to Denis Thatcher in 1951 and her twins arrived in 1953. At the crossroads in the woods, she chose family for this period of her life and stepped away from her young career. When the twins were ready for school, she again chose work for the next phase of her life. Elected to Parliament in 1959, she rose steadily through the party ranks and was named Prime Minister a quick 20 years later in 1979 – becoming Britain's first female Prime Minister.

When she finally stepped down as Conservative Leader in 1990, to pursue some much-deserved time for self with Denis and her grown twins, Thatcher left behind a world transformed. The British economy had rebounded with a new confidence, the Soviet Union had collapsed, democracy was once again striding across the globe and she had survived an assassination attempt by the Irish Republican Army.

What a superb example for us all to strive for and achieve W•F•S Balance despite the many challenges and temptations the world provides.

# W·F·S Balance Developmental Action

**Developmental Purpose:**

The purpose of this seven-day *W·F·S Balance Development Action Phase* is to:

- Better understand W·F·S Balance;
- Explore your current W·F·S Balance percentages;
- Identify where your W·F·S Balance percentages should be, and
- Take action to achieve your appropriate W·F·S Balance.

## Journaling

Journal these 7 days with a focus on the W·F·S balancing actions in your daily activities.

The first day of this developmental period, stop and capture your W·F·S balancing actions for each previous hour. As you journal, label your activities as W, F, or S. Likewise, as you journal, please take particular care to capture the emotions, surprises, and new insights you experience and gain.

After one full day, tally your W·F·S activities. Then analyze the results to determine your current ratio of activities. Plot your balance in box below:

| Current W·F·S Balance | | |
|:---:|:---:|:---:|
| **Work** | **Family** | **Self** |
| % | % | % |

## Semi-Structured Conversations:

To assist in identifying your current W·F·S Balance, hold semi-structured conversations with:

- Yourself,
- Your significant other, and
- A leader you consider especially W·F·S Balanced (preferably not your Mentor).

Prior to the conversations, observe your subjects and document in your journal the W·F·S Balance you see in their day-to-day actions.

At the beginning of the conversations, summarize the philosophy of Courageous Leadership and the W•F•S Balance for the interviewee.

During the conversations, capture the findings in your journal. Questions for these conversations might include:

- How important is achieving W•F•S Balance?
- What is the appropriate W•F•S Balance for me at this stage in my life and career?
- Can I truly balance W•F•S while striving for professional excellence?

In your journal, verbally identify the differences between your observed W•F•S Balance and desired W•F•S Balance so that you may begin closing the gaps.

**A.I.R. Hot Wash:**
Schedule a conversation with your Mentor to discuss:

- **Advice**: What advice does he/she have for you regarding W•F•S Balance in general – and specifically your W•F•S Balance.
- **Information**: As your Mentor for sources of additional information that they have found useful regarding W•F•S Balance.
- **Referrals**: Ask who should you speak to further about W•F•S Balance.

In your journal, verbally identify the differences between your observed W•F•S Balance and desired W•F•S Balance so that you may begin closing the gaps.

With your identified W•F•S Balance and the conversations accomplished, now is the time to identify your appropriate W•F•S Balance:

| Appropriate W•F•S Balance | | |
|---|---|---|
| **Work** | **Family** | **Self** |
| % | % | % |

**W•F•S Culminating Actions**: Given the identified gap between your current W•F•S Balance and desired W•F•S Balance:

- Include *W•F•S Balancing* in your IDP. Identify developmental goals and activities. Developmental activities may include training (classroom, on-line, webinar), mentoring (either being a mentor or protégé), college courses, books (including audiobooks), developmental projects, stretch assignments, job shadowing, job rotation, networking opportunities, conferences, etc.
- Review and, if needed, modify your draft IMS to match your current understanding of W•F•S Balance.
- Adjust your life and calendar accordingly to achieve this desired W•F•S Balance so that you may fulfill your IMS.

**7-Day Summary:**
During this seven-day *W•F•S Balance Development Action Phase*, you have:

- Conducted in-depth self-reflection;
- Held semi-structured conversations with significant people in your personal and professional lives;
- Sought advice, information, & referrals from your Mentor;
- Captured your emotions, surprises, and new insights from these 7 days of development in your journal;
- Identified your appropriate W•F•S Balance for this time in your life;
- Identified actions to successfully implement your courageous W•F•S Balance;
- Added *W•F•S Balance* to your IDP; and
- Took the initial steps to adjust your life and calendar to meet that W•F•S Balance.

**Bottom Line Value Creation:**

- Now balancing your W•F•S at the correct levels of commitment for your life and career at this time, with inputs and support from significant people in your life and career, you now possess an agreed upon mix of work, family, and self that permits undistracted fulfillment of your IMS.

For each characteristic below, select the descriptor score that best matches your current knowledge level

| Characteristic | Score 0-10 |
|---|---|
| Principled | |
| TCE | |
| WFS | |
| Vision | |
| Humility | |
| Powerful | |
| Bold | |
| Driven | |
| Charismatic | |
| Unreasonable | |
| Total Score: | |

| Score | Descriptors |
|---|---|
| 0 | You are unaware of this characteristic as a value-added part of leadership |
| 1 | You have just learned about this characteristic |
| 2 | You know about this characteristic but do not yet understand its value to your leadership |
| 3 | You understand the value of this characteristic but are not yet prepared to purposefully exhibit it |
| 4 | You understand the value of this characteristic and uneasily try to exhibit it when you remember |
| 5 | You understand the value of this characteristic and comfortably exhibit it when you remember |
| 6 | You comfortably exhibit this characteristic on almost all occasions |
| 7 | You recognize the growth of this characteristic in yourself and are naturally and confidently exhibiting it as a central part of your leadership |
| 8 | You are recognized by others for this characteristic as a particular strength |
| 9 | You comfortably mentor others in exhbiting this characteristic |
| 10 | You are the ideal example of this characteristic |

Now that you have completed your seven days of *W•F•S Balancing* development, let's take a snapshot of your knowledge level. After you assess your current level of knowledge per the matrix above, look back at your Day-Zero level of *W•F•S Balancing* knowledge. We would expect that your level has increased due to your developmental actions.

# COURAGEOUS CHARACTERISTIC 4: VISIONARY

*All dream, but not equally. Those who dream by night in the dusty recesses of their minds, wake in the day to find that it was vanity: but the dreamers of the day are dangerous, for they may act on their dreams with open eyes, to make them possible.*
  -T.E. Lawrence

Who knew "Lawrence of Arabia" (aka T.E. Lawrence) was a poet? Among his many courageous accomplishments on the battlefield, T.E. Lawrence was also a renowned author and poet – most notably for his seminal work entitled "Seven Pillars of Wisdom" – thereby demonstrating his courageous leadership in multiple forms.

## *I am a Courageous Leader… therefore, I am Visionary!*

Courageous leaders are visionary *Dreamers of Day* – as they dream with their eyes open to make their dreams reality. Within the leadership academic literature, vision is THE most frequently cited characteristic of leaders. In practice, being a Visionary Courageous Leader first requires the willingness & ability to think many years into the future and then take actions today and every day to make those visions a reality.

By definition, goals are the broadly generalized statements of your desired future – with strong clarity but short on details – that boldly imagine a new "realm of the possible." Where do you want to be in 30 years? Are you retired and living in the Caribbean? Are you the CEO of a Fortune 500 company? Are you a philanthropist?

There is no right or wrong answers, for each of us gets to envision our own futures.

Don't be intimidated by the blank page if you haven't yet thought much about what you want for dinner tonight, let alone what you want to achieve in your time on earth. But now is the time to start thinking and writing about just that – regardless of your age or position. Begin to sketch out your visionary goals in broad terms. Don't worry too much about the details as the details will come later.

In order to be visionary and have the time to enact your visions, your T•C•E Alignment and W•F•S Balance must support your vision. Regarding T•C•E Alignment, make educating yourself – formally and informally – part of your alignment; mature your thinking about work – and where it fits into your vision. Regarding W•F•S Balance, make sure you include people who are important to you in your visionary thinking and writing – especially if they will be involved in the execution of your vision. Make sure you plan for balance as you envision – recognizing that certain periods of your life are going to be heavily out of balance.

Ultimately, vision is the characteristic that separates leaders from managers. Managers, even the best in the world, simply act on lifeless *things* using highly reliable processes and mostly predictable outcomes – risk for them is routinely measurable to the third decimal place. Leaders, on the other hand, tell visionary stories to *people* (each of whom has their own life's dreams) and convinces these *people* to join them on their fanciful voyages to far off distant places.

Acting on visions is the part where courage quickly becomes especially relevant – as you will, probably for the first time, express to someone other than yourself what you are all about. I will never forget the first time I dropped my life's vision on my wife, and I will certainly never forget the look on her face as we sat at lunch, with our new baby beside us. But, then it was out there, in the open, shared – and much harder to renege than my vain dreams of night.

I recommend setting vision goals for the next thirty years[3] at 30-year, 10-year, and 1-year milestones. We go in reverse order as our 30-year goals will inform our 10-year goals which will then inform 1-year goals. After identifying your goals, you must then

---

[3] Even when you are relatively late in your career, as I am at this writing, you should still project 30 years to envision what you wish to leave behind.

translate these visionary *desires* into concrete objectives that will serve as the mile markers to measure your progress. Goals are fuzzy – while objectives are the concrete milestones necessary to achieve your goals. Graduating from college is a goal while identifying, selecting, and completing 24 disparate undergraduate courses are objectives that achieve that goal.

From my own *Courageous Leadership* experiences, my youngest daughter was married the day before Easter this spring. As a consequence, we had a large number of friends and family over for Easter brunch the next morning – along with their dozens of children. As a part of the festivities, we hid hundreds of Easter eggs throughout our front yard. With the children all assembled in the back yard, it was my responsibility to herd them all to the front yard in an orderly fashion – but that plan was immediately dashed as the children began running full throttle toward the "hidden" eggs. As I watched them stream by me, on an absolutely glorious afternoon – all laughing, jumping, and screaming with delight – I was momentarily overcome with emotion – because I was watching in real-time the fulfillment of a vision I had seen in my head dozens of times over the past thirty years. For there was my family, friends, children, and grand-children; celebrating life together; in our home – and all the worries of the day were swept away. And the dozens of years of planning, working, and worrying were infinitely rewarded before my very eyes.

# Zhang Xin

**4**

Self-made billionaire Zhang Xin courageously followed her personal and professional vision for a new life and a new China, thus delivering herself from living in a small single room with her mother at the age of 14 to developing 54 million square feet of prime office real estate in Beijing and Shanghai. Known as "the woman who built Beijing," Zhang is one of the most celebrated and successful commercial real estate developers in China. With her company SOHO China, she has transformed the architectural landscape of Beijing and Shanghai.

Zhang was born in 1965, just before Mao Zedong's Cultural Revolution, which relocated capitalists and intellectuals to the countryside for "re-education" purposes. Her parents, as university graduates, were relocated with their young daughter to a life of working in the fields. When Zhang was eight, her mother was allowed to return to Hong Kong where she worked as a translator while Zhang slept on her mother's desk, using her large dictionary as a pillow. When Zhang was old enough, she began working in sweat shops, eventually saving enough money to take her 1st step (of many to follow) toward a vision for a better life – a one-way ticket to London. Zhang said in a 60 Minutes interview that when she arrived, she was so overwhelmed by the noise and lights that she sat on her suitcase and cried. Her first job in London was working in a fish and chips stand, which obviously didn't pay much but provide

---

plenty to eat. Zhang again saved enough money toward another major step in her life vision – English language instruction. With her new language and sustained hard work, Zhang eventually won a scholarship to Sussex University (another step in her life's vision) where she earned a bachelor's degree in Economics. Zhang continued her studies, earning a master's degree in Development Economics from Cambridge University (accomplishing another step).

Founding SOHO was exceptionally and simply yet another step toward her life's vision of transforming her own life and that of her homeland. Exceptionally, for its profound scope and success – but simultaneously simple, for it was merely the next logical progression in Zhang's personal and professional vision. When we map our own life visions, we can also make such simultaneously exceptional and simple choices and actions.

# Vision Developmental Action

**Developmental Purpose:**

The purpose of this seven-day *Vision-Development Action Phase* is to:

- Better understand vision;
- Bring to life your personal and professional vision;
- Identify the Lifetime Goals & Objectives needed to realize your vision; and
- Take courageous action to achieve your vision.

**Journal:**

Journal these 7 days with a focus on your vision actions across your day-to-day activities. Draft your initial Daily, 1, 10, and 30-year vision* goals and their relative objectives in your journal. This initial vision should not be overly complicated as it simply identifies general themes regarding what you want to achieve. Identify both personal and professional goals.

| GOAL 1: EDUCATE MY CHILDREN | | |
|---|---|---|
| **Timeline** | **Goal** | **Objectives** |
| 30-Year | My Children are all College Graduates | Financing is in Place to Fund four degrees |
| 10-Year | My Children are all High School Graduates with strong GPAs and varied extra-curricular activities | All accepted to universities of their choice |
| 1-Year | My Children are on a path to becoming well-rounded students | Spend time tutoring my Children Enroll them in extra-curricular activities |
| Today | My children are in school today | Dress them Feed them breakfast Get them on the bus |

*Each distinct vision goal should have its own table showing its own objectives. Be careful not to identify too many vision goals as spreading your vision too thinly will make it difficult to obtain any of your goals.*

We work backwards from 30 years, as the farthest goals & objectives will inform and enable the nearer ones. Remember, goals are abstract while objectives are tangible. Likewise, the farther in the future the goal or objective, the less detail needed. Duplicate this framework for each of your life goals. As a rule of thumb, you should initially identify 1-3 life goals so that you are thorough without being scattered. You should then identify the tangible objectives that you will accomplish to fulfill the goals. Like the IMS, this LG&O Vision framework should be simply stated but with the deep thought and self-reflection a document of this magnitude requires.

As you journal, please take particular care to capture the emotions, surprises, and new insights you experience and gain.

As you journal, verbally identify the differences between your observed vision and desired vision so that you may begin closing the gaps.

## Semi-Structured Conversations:

To assist in identifying your vision, hold three semi-structured conversations with:

1) Yourself;
2) Your significant other; and
3) A leader you consider especially visionary (preferably not your Mentor).

Prior to the conversations, observe your subjects and document in your journal the vision you see in their day-to-day actions.

At the beginning of the conversations, summarize the philosophy of Courageous Leadership and vision for the interviewee.

During the conversations, capture the findings in your journal. As you journal, please take particular care to capture the emotions, surprises, and new insights you experience and gain.

Questions for these conversations might include:

- What personal and professional goals do I want to accomplish in the next 30, 10, and 1 years?

- What are the related objectives I must accomplish at each milestone to fulfill these goals? How much time, money, and other resources are required to meet my objectives?
- What do I need to start doing today to meet these objectives?
- What do I need to stop doing today to meet these objectives?

In your journal, verbally identify the differences between your observed vision and desired vision so that you may begin closing the gaps.

**A.I.R. Hot Wash:**
Schedule a conversation with your Mentor to discuss A.I.R.
- **Advice**: What advice does he/she have for you regarding vision in general – and specifically your vision.
- **Information**: Ask your Mentor for sources of additional information that they have found useful regarding vision.
- **Referrals**: Ask who you should speak to further about vision.

In your journal, verbally identify the differences between your observed vision and desired vision so that you may begin closing the gaps.

**Vision Culminating Actions**: Given the identified gap between your current vision and desired vision:
- Include *Courageous Vision Development* in your IDP. Identify developmental goals and activities. Developmental activities may include training (classroom, on-line, webinar), mentoring (either being a mentor or protégé), college courses, books (including audiobooks), developmental projects, stretch assignments, job shadowing, job rotation, networking opportunities, conferences, etc.
- Review and, if needed, modify your draft IMS to match your current understanding of vision.
- Adjust your life and calendar accordingly to achieve this desired Courageous Vision so that you may fulfill your IMS.
- Review and update (as needed) your W•F•S Balance & T•C•E Alignment.

**7-Day Summary:**

During this seven-day *Vision Development Action Phase*, you have:

- Conducted in-depth self-reflection regarding your 30-year, 10-year, and 1-year goals & objectives;
- Held semi-structured conversations with significant people in your personal and professional lives;
- Sought advice, information, & referrals from your Mentor;
- Captured your emotions, surprises, and new insights from these 7 days of development in your journal;
- Identified actions to successfully implement your courageous vision;
- Taken the initial steps to adjust your life and calendar to meet that vision; and
- Updated as needed your IMS, IDP, W•F•S Balance, & T•C•E Alignment.

**Bottom Line Value Creation:**

- Looking far ahead with your 1, 10, and 30 Year draft goals & objectives identified, you have a clear path visible to accomplish your lifetime goals and therefore fulfill your IMS.

For each characteristic below, select the descriptor score that best matches your current knowledge level

| Characteristic | Score 0-10 |
|---|---|
| **Principled** | |
| **TCE** | |
| **WFS** | |
| **Vision** | |
| **Humility** | |
| **Powerful** | |
| **Bold** | |
| **Driven** | |
| **Charismatic** | |
| **Unreasonable** | |
| **Total Score:** | |

| Score | Descriptors |
|---|---|
| **0** | You are unaware of this characteristic as a value-added part of leadership |
| **1** | You have just learned about this characteristic |
| **2** | You know about this characteristic but do not yet understand its value to your leadership |
| **3** | You understand the value of this characteristic but are not yet prepared to purposefully exhibit it |
| **4** | You understand the value of this characteristic and uneasily try to exhibit it when you remember |
| **5** | You understand the value of this characteristic and comfortably exhibit it when you remember |
| **6** | You comfortably exhibit this characteristic on almost all occasions |
| **7** | You recognize the growth of this characteristic in yourself and are naturally and confidently exhibiting it as a central part of your leadership |
| **8** | You are recognized by others for this characteristic as a particular strength |
| **9** | You comfortably mentor others in exhbiting this characteristic |
| **10** | You are the ideal example of this characteristic |

Now that you have completed your seven days of *vision* development, let's take a snapshot of your knowledge level. After you assess your current level of knowledge per the matrix above, look back at your Day-Zero level of *vision* knowledge. We would expect that your level has increased due to your developmental actions.

# COURAGEOUS CHARACTERISTIC 5: HUMBLE

*In my walks, everyone I meet is my superior in some way, and in that I learn from them.*
-Ralph Waldo Emerson

## I am a Courageous Leader... therefore, I am Humble!

*Courageous Leaders* purposefully develop and sustain a genuine humility within themselves, their teams, and their organizations that truly recognizes the value contributions of all with whom they interact. They do in fact *learn from everyone they meet* because they are humble enough to open their hearts and minds to everyone they meet.

This humility is grounded in their recognition that they are the exception – gifted with the seeds of *willingness & ability* to lead. For, this seemingly simple intersection of energy and talent is exceedingly rare – bestowed upon a fortunate few. You are probably one of those gifted few! Therefore, when leading, these humble leaders execute their responsibilities with empathy, calmness, and grace.

Further, these humble leaders accept the leadership obligation that comes with being the willing and able exceptions. They organize, plan, and execute without reservation simply because the work must be done – and they are willing and able. They recognize, that to maximize their value contribution to themselves, their teams, and their organizations, they must regularly be willing to be *2nd Best* – purposefully surrounding themselves with people more technically, cognitively, and emotionally capable.

Of course, we can all easily recall "Leaders" from history and from our own experiences that do not fit this "*Humble*" description. The kinds of egotistical, arrogant people who almost everyone dislikes but who, nonetheless, realize outward "success" due to their achievements. These people convince millions of their followers to commit genocide and lead their country to war for personal glorification or riches.

But, in my definition of *Courageous Leadership*, such tyrannical activities are NOT leadership. Stated in another way, *Courageous Leadership* and tyranny are mutually exclusive as they cannot exist in the same place at the same time. When a person chooses tyranny – they abandon their leadership roles and responsibilities. The fine line in the sand between tyranny and leadership comes down to humility!

Let's back up for a second. What is your purpose in life as a *Courageous Leader*? So far, we have talked about the characteristics of being principled, T•C•E Aligned, W•F•S Balanced, visionary – and now humble. What is the common theme between these characteristics? In my mind, the common theme is that these characteristics maximize the value of your teams and organizations through concurrently maximizing the value of your own life and the lives of those on your teams and within your organizations.

If you are an admirer of the Nobel Laureate Milton Friedman, you may say the purpose of your life is to maximize profits! And I would likely agree with you and Mr. Friedman – but I would also tell you, as would Mr. Friedman, that profit maximization (or performance maximization for non-profits) is not a straight-line path. You don't maximize profits/performance by killing either yourself or your team. Rather, you maximize profits and performance by humbly leading yourself and your teams.

Thanksgiving is a big deal in our house! It is both an occasion to give thanks and a rare opportunity to get the entire "herd" together. We have a mini-United Nations every year with our combined biological, in-law, and surrogate family. Thanksgiving this year was no different – except for one small hiccup.

Sometime in the late afternoon – between dinner and dessert – the sinks began gurgling and backing up. And we had over forty people in our home. While plunging various sinks and toilets, I first smelled and then saw sewage backing up in my bedroom shower. As a trained investigator, I quickly surmised I had either a blockage or an over-filled septic system. To prevent further disruption, I called both a septic system drainer and a plumber. They arrived simultaneously and began working on their respective tasks. The plumber, Carlos, quickly located a blocked drain line and "snaked" it open in a matter of seconds. So, with his work done and his Thanksgiving already interrupted, he and I were watching the septic system drainer, Joe, do his work.

After a few seconds of watching the large suction hose vacuum up various substances, Carlos exclaimed "Oh my God, what is that?" as a blob of some material bobbed to the surface. Joe, being the philosopher septic tank drainer that he obviously is, remarked without pause "I stopped asking what it was a long time ago – and now accept that it just is!"

So, there was Emerson's principle writ large! Who would have ever expected on a chilly Thanksgiving evening, with the sun going down, while waiting for my dessert to be served, I would learn a life's lesson from Joe the Philosopher! *"It Just Is!"*

# Harry Truman

Harry Truman is often called the "Accidental President" as he was not the first choice to be Vice-President under Franklin Delano Roosevelt. Actually, he was not expected to ever be in the White House at all. But on April 12, 1945, less than three months into his term as Vice-President, Harry Truman became the 33$^{rd}$ President of the United States upon Roosevelt's death. Unprepared, and unsuspecting of his fate, President Truman surrounded himself with the most highly qualified personnel he could find.

Upon assuming the office of the Presidency, Truman humbly asked Roosevelt's cabinet to stay as he recognized the immediate need to keep these men who possessed unique skills and critical information that fueled the high-speed train he was now leading. To a man, no one in Roosevelt's cabinet respected the new President – but Truman humbly put the needs of the country above his own ego.

Once he got his footing as President, Truman began surrounding himself with the most competent and capable people he could find – following the tried and tested leadership tenet of not needing to be the smartest or most capable person in the room. Among his eventual cabinet picks was retired Army General, George Marshall, whom Truman nominated for Secretary of State – the most prestigious and highly visible of all cabinet posts. Marshall was a Five Star General and the Army Chief of Staff and had orchestrated the largest military expansion in U.S. history. Winston Churchill dubbed him "the organizer of victory" for his leadership in World War II. His accomplishments were monumental and his popularity with the American people far exceeded Truman's. When Truman was asked why he would pick a man such as Marshall to serve under him when "George Marshall is more qualified than you to be President!" Truman humbly replied, "George Marshall is more qualified than me to be the President, but I am the President and I need him on my team."

That kind of humility is both rare and invaluable – and a worthy ideal for us to follow.

# Humility Developmental Action

**Developmental Purpose:**

The purpose of this seven-day *Humility-Development Action Phase* is to:

- Look both inward and outward regarding humility;
- Better understand humility and its place in your personal and professional lives;
- Identify your current level of humility;
- Compare that finding to where you could/should be; and
- Take courageous action to close the gap.

## Journaling

Journal these 7 days with a focus on your observations of humility in your day-to-day actions. As your journal, please take special care to capture the emotions, surprises, and new insights you experience and gain.

As you journal, verbally identify the differences between your observed humility and desired humility so that you may begin closing the gaps.

During these 7 days you may want to focus on the following questions while journaling.

- What steps are you taking to truly appreciate and value the people who work on your team? Think about the strengths and weaknesses of each person on your team.
- Think about a leader who is humble. What actions, behaviors or attitudes reflect their humility? Why do people like working for them?
- What are some possible outcomes and benefits of being humble?
- Think about a time when you realized that you may have achieved a better outcome if you had listened, paused to reflect, assumed the best of another person and given respect to another person.
- Notice when you esteem someone and when you diminish someone. Also, notice when you feel esteemed or diminished. What are the outcomes?

**Semi-Structured Conversations:**

A good way to study humility is across generational lines. Thus, for this developmental phase, you are going to conduct semi-structured conversations about humility with each working generation (interview yourself for your own generation).

| Generation | Birth Range |
| --- | --- |
| Baby Boomers | 1943-1964 |
| Generation X | 1965-1979 |
| Millennials | 1980-2000 |
| Generation Z | 2001-Present |

Prior to the conversations, observe your subjects and document in your journal the humility you see in their day-to-day actions.

At the beginning of the conversations, summarize the philosophy of Courageous Leadership and humility for the interviewee.

During the conversations, capture the findings in your journal. As you journal, please take particular care to capture the emotions, surprises, and new insights you experience and gain. Questions for these conversations might include:

- What are your views on humility in your personal and professional lives?
- How humble are the other working generations?
- Identify the core differences between the generations.
- What are the core similarities?
- Are the differences in generations foundational or just bothersome?
- What steps have you taken to truly appreciate and value the people you work with?

In your journal, verbally identify the differences between your observed humility and desired humility so that you may begin closing the gaps.

**A.I.R. Hot Wash:**

Schedule a conversation with your Mentor to discuss A.I.R.

- **Advice**: What advice does he/she have for you regarding humility in general – and specifically your level of humility.

- **Information**: Ask your Mentor for sources of additional information that they have found useful regarding humility.
- **Referrals**: Ask who you should speak to further about humility.
- In your journal, verbally identify the differences between your observed humility and desired humility so that you may begin closing the gaps.

**Humility Culminating Actions**:

Given the identified gap between your current humility and desired humility:

- Include *Courageous Humility Development* in your IDP. Identify developmental goals and activities. Developmental activities may include training (classroom, on-line, webinar), mentoring (either being a mentor or protégé), college courses, books (including audiobooks), developmental projects, stretch assignments, job shadowing, job rotation, networking opportunities, conferences, etc.
- Review and, if needed, modify your draft IMS to match your current understanding of humility.
- Adjust your life and calendar accordingly to achieve this desired Courageous Humility so that you may fulfill your IMS.
- Review and update as needed your W•F•S Balance & T•C•E Alignment.

**7-Day Summary:**

During this seven-day *Humility Development Action Phase*, you have:

- Conducted in-depth self-reflection;
- Held semi-structured conversations with each of the working generations;
- Sought advice, information, & referrals from your Mentor;
- Captured your emotions, surprises, and new insights from these 7 days of development in your journal;
- Measured your current level of humility;
- Identified actions to achieve Courageous Humility;
- Taken the initial steps to achieve Courageous Humility; and

- Updated as needed your IMS, IDP, W•F•S Balance, & T•C•E Alignment.

**Bottom Line Value Creation:**
- Recognizing the value of surrounding yourself with competent and capable professionals, you can use your Courageous Humility to compel them to even greater heights of excellence.

For each characteristic below, select the descriptor score that best matches your current knowledge level

| Characteristic | Score 0-10 |
|---|---|
| **Principled** | |
| **TCE** | |
| **WFS** | |
| **Vision** | |
| **Humility** | |
| **Powerful** | |
| **Bold** | |
| **Driven** | |
| **Charismatic** | |
| **Unreasonable** | |
| **Total Score:** | |

| Score | Descriptors |
|---|---|
| 0 | You are unaware of this characteristic as a value-added part of leadership |
| 1 | You have just learned about this characteristic |
| 2 | You know about this characteristic but do not yet understand its value to your leadership |
| 3 | You understand the value of this characteristic but are not yet prepared to purposefully exhibit it |
| 4 | You understand the value of this characteristic and uneasily try to exhibit it when you remember |
| 5 | You understand the value of this characteristic and comfortably exhibit it when you remember |
| 6 | You comfortably exhibit this characteristic on almost all occasions |
| 7 | You recognize the growth of this characteristic in yourself and are naturally and confidently exhibiting it as a central part of your leadership |
| 8 | You are recognized by others for this characteristic as a particular strength |
| 9 | You comfortably mentor others in exhibiting this characteristic |
| 10 | You are the ideal example of this characteristic |

Now that you have completed your seven days of *humility* development, let's take a snapshot of your knowledge level. After you assess your current level of knowledge per the matrix above, look back at your Day-Zero level of *humility* knowledge. We would expect that your level has increased due to your developmental actions.

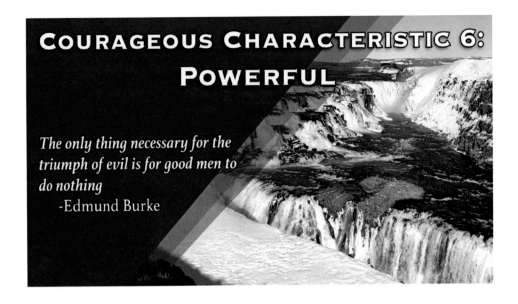

*The only thing necessary for the triumph of evil is for good men to do nothing*
-Edmund Burke

## *I am a Courageous Leader... therefore, I am Powerful!*

Under the scientific principal of entropy, left to its own design, the world tends toward disorder. Weeds encroach your yard without proper attention; ships rust without constant chipping and painting; and evil fills any vacuum left void of good. As power is the only means through which leaders can enact their vision, *Courageous Leaders* must voluntarily create, collect, and use power to control entropy and create value.

Power is defined as the willingness & ability to influence the actions of self, teams, & organizations. It is generally created, collected, and used in seven ways:

1) <u>Positional</u> – your position suggests that others should adhere to your intent
2) <u>Expertise</u> – you have valuable knowledge, skills, or abilities
3) <u>Information</u> – you possess scarce, valuable insights
4) <u>Coercive</u> – you can inflict pain, harm, or death
5) <u>Reward</u> – you can reward with money, gifts, etc.
6) <u>Connection</u> – you can introduce people to other's they want to know
7) <u>Referent</u> – others admire your leadership characteristics and want to follow you

Regardless of the type of power, all seven are voluntarily given to the leader. Members of the team either do or do not respect the hierarchy of the organization; respect your expertise; desire your potential rewards, etc. Even when coercive power is used – hopefully only in the rarest of circumstances during short periods of duress – the recipient of the coercion can choose to either accept the leader's intent or accept the resulting pain, harm, or death.

Speaking of time spans, referent power, is the only use of power that is sustainable over time as all others eventually lose their ability to positively influence. You can only say "Because I am the boss – that's why!" so many times; expertise, information, and connections can be replicated by others; rewards provide short-term influence on the margins; and coercion becomes tyranny if used excessively. Thus, referent power is the ideal means through which courageous leaders strive to lead.

Establishing a Courageous Vision requires that you influence others to pursue that vision with you. Courageous Power is how you unapologetically impart your will on those who volunteer to follow you. Given the ideal of referent power, *Courageous Leadership* is therefore, voluntary in both directions – as you must be willing to lead, and your team must be willing to follow. Of course, you can be forced through coercion and/or circumstance to fill a leadership position – but you must then voluntary to accept the responsibilities of true *Courageous Leadership* – otherwise you will simply manage your team as a lifeless "resource" rather than leading them as living, breathing, thinking human beings. Likewise, those on your team can be forced to follow your directions – usually then even only in the short term. But to truly "follow" you and give you 100% of their potential, they must commit themselves to your leadership voluntarily.

As power is always given by the follower and referent power is the ultimate objective, leaders must ensure their teams and organizations understand the linkages between the other types of power and referent power. For example, in the rare instances when coercive power is appropriate and used, the team must willingly accept that the short-term coercive action is in their long-term best interest. This linkage between powers is created by sufficiently communicating what is acceptable and not acceptable through implicit culture and explicit objectives prior to the coercive action.

The same is true for the other powers – the follower must understand how your use of power is ultimately in their best interest.

Regarding ability, you must constantly hone your T•C•E Alignment to ensure you are using the right power at the right time – always with an eye on maturing to referent power as your primary power. As you examine the types of power, you will notice they span the T•C•E gamut – with referent almost entirely within the realm of emotional intelligence.

Finally, given the idea that referent power is the ideal power, I state again that *Courageous Leadership* and tyranny are mutually exclusive, as they can never exist in the same place at the same time – either you are a leader or you are a tyrant – you cannot be both. Tyrants coerce while leaders convince; tyrants oppress while leaders empower; tyrants threaten while leaders encourage; leaders serve the better good while tyrants serve themselves. Thus, ultimately, Courageous Leaders unapologetically create, collect, and use power to achieve their personal and professional vision on behalf of those in their charge.

One of the great joys of owning a business is possessing the awesome power of creating jobs. As I enter the second half of my life, with my children raised and out of the house, this ability is now one of my top priorities. On the flip side, a business owner also has the power – and sometimes the responsibility – to take a job from someone. With nearly two decades in the CEO Chair, I have had the misfortune of using my power of termination on multiple unpleasant occasions. In fact, I have terminated people with whom I served in combat; I have terminated people with whom I had been friends for over twenty years; and I have terminated people for which I had the utmost personal respect. All these actions were done with considerable soul-searching; all with great anguish; and all with significant sadness. But none with regret! For, upon assuming the role of CEO, I promised myself that I would never permit my team to suffer because I was unwilling to take the necessary actions to best serve my team.

# Pope Saint John Paul II

5

There are 1.2 billion Roman Catholics worldwide and they all look to the *"Bishop of Rome"* also known as the Pope for not only spiritual guidance, but also leadership. Karol Josef Wojtyla, known to the world as "John Paul II," began his tenure as Pope on October 16, 1978. At aged 58, he was the youngest Pope for over 100 years and the first Pope from outside Italy in 455 years.

John Paul II was born in the Polish town of Wadowice, the youngest of three children. As a teenager, he enrolled in Jagiellonian University, but his studies were interrupted when the Nazis invaded Poland in 1939. After the eventual defeat of Germany in 1945, Europe was carved up between the allies and the Soviet Union was given control of Poland and other neighboring countries. For John Paul II, this transition was simply exchanging one form of tyranny for another. His personal courage displayed through his public writings, suggested a conservative interpretation of religious doctrine, which made the young priest quite powerful inside the Polish church and further afield.

By 1978 he was a Cardinal and the leading Catholic figure in Poland as well as a growing force in Rome. This led to his election to Pope, but on the eighth ballot as the compromise candidate between the traditionalists and the liberals. Despite this fact, he

5 By Dennis Jarvis- CC BY 2.0, https://www.flickr.com/photos/archer10/12727135684

boldly stepped into the role without hesitation – and began immediately creating, collecting and using the power his new position afforded.

His election posed a significant dilemma for the communist rulers in both Warsaw and Moscow as his writings were a direct challenge to the communists who disavowed God and believed there was no higher power than the state to whom the people owed absolute allegiance. However, his powerful actions as Pope quickly absolved the communists of any choices as he immediately embarked on a major evangelical effort that involved traveling to 129 countries (his arrival always marked by his kneeling and kissing the ground) and spreading the gospel of faith and inclusion.

John Paul II died on April 2, 2005 after a short illness just a few days short of his 85th birthday after nearly 30 years as Pope. During that time, he evolved his power from positional to referent – and was beloved the world over. As he was unafraid to use his power, he left a lasting legacy during a time of great transition in the world. His use of power helped destroy tyranny and replaced it with leadership.

## Power Developmental Action

### Developmental Purpose:

The purpose of this seven-day *Power-Development Action Phase* is to:

- Better understand the need to create, collect, and use power;
- Identify your current level of power;
- Compare that finding to where you could/should be; and
- Take courageous action to close the gap.

### Journaling

As a reminder, the commonly discussed types of power are:

- Position  - Information  - Reward  - Punishment
  - Expert   - Connection  - Referent

Journal these 7 days with a focus on your observations of power actions in your day-to-day actions. As you journal, please take special care to capture the emotions, surprises, and new insights you experience and gain.

As you journal, verbally identify the differences between your observed power and desired power so that you may begin closing the gaps.

**Semi-Structured Conversations:**
Have a semi-structured conversation with:
- Yourself,
- A leader you consider especially powerful (preferably not your Mentor).

Prior to the conversations, observe your subject and document in your journal the power you see in their day-to-day actions.

At the beginning of the conversation, summarize the philosophy of Courageous Leadership and the powerful characteristic for the interviewee.

During the conversation, capture the findings in your journal. Please take special care to capture the emotions, surprises, and new insights you experience and gain. Questions for this conversation might include:
- What is your "go-to" power and why?
- What power(s) do they avoid and why?
- How do they differentiate between power & tyranny?
- In what types of situations have you used each of the forms of power identified above? What were the outcomes?
- Think of a leader you admire. What kind of power does he/she use?
- Think of a time when you effectively used referent power. What was the outcome?
- What do you do to encourage people to want to follow you as a leader?

In your journal, verbally identify the differences between your observed power and desired power so that you may begin closing the gaps.

**A.I.R. Hot Wash:**
Schedule a conversation with your Mentor to discuss A.I.R.

- **Advice**: What advice does he/she have for you regarding power in general – and specifically your level of power.
- **Information**: Ask your Mentor for sources of additional information that they have found useful regarding power.
- **Referrals**: Ask who you should speak to further about power.

In your journal, verbally identify the differences between your observed power and desired power so that you may begin closing the gaps.

**Power Culminating Actions**: Given the identified gap between your current power and desired power:

- Include *Courageous Powerful Development* in your IDP. Identify developmental goals and activities. Developmental activities may include training (classroom, on-line, webinar), mentoring (either being a mentor or protégé), college courses, books (including audiobooks), developmental projects, stretch assignments, job shadowing, job rotation, networking opportunities, conferences, etc.
- Review and, if needed, modify your draft IMS to match your current understanding of power.
- Adjust your life and calendar accordingly to achieve this desired Courageous Power so that you may fulfill your IMS.
- Review and update as needed your W•F•S Balance & T•C•E Alignment.

**7-Day Summary:**
During this seven-day *Power Development Action Phase*, you have:

- Conducted in-depth self-reflection;
- Held a semi-structured conversation with a "Powerful" leader;
- Sought advice, information, & referrals from your Mentor;
- Captured your emotions, surprises, and new insights from these 7 days of development in your journal;
- Measured your current level of power;

- Identified actions to achieve Courageous Power;
- Taken the initial steps to achieve Courageous Power; and
- Updated (as needed) your IMS, IDP, W•F•S Balance, & T•C•E Alignment.

**Bottom Line Value Creation:**
- With your understanding of the need to create, collect, and use Courageous Power on behalf of yourself, your family, your team, and your organizations, you possess the influence needed to impart your will – thereby creating value and avoiding chaos.

For each characteristic below, select the descriptor score that best matches your current knowledge level

| Characteristic | Score 0-10 |
|---|---|
| **Principled** | |
| **TCE** | |
| **WFS** | |
| **Vision** | |
| **Humility** | |
| **Powerful** | |
| **Bold** | |
| **Driven** | |
| **Charismatic** | |
| **Unreasonable** | |
| **Total Score:** | |

| Score | Descriptors |
|---|---|
| **0** | You are unaware of this characteristic as a value-added part of leadership |
| **1** | You have just learned about this characteristic |
| **2** | You know about this characteristic but do not yet understand its value to your leadership |
| **3** | You understand the value of this characteristic but are not yet prepared to purposefully exhibit it |
| **4** | You understand the value of this characteristic and uneasily try to exhibit it when you remember |
| **5** | You understand the value of this characteristic and comfortably exhibit it when you remember |
| **6** | You comfortably exhibit this characteristic on almost all occasions |
| **7** | You recognize the growth of this characteristic in yourself and are naturally and confidently exhibiting it as a central part of your leadership |
| **8** | You are recognized by others for this characteristic as a particular strength |
| **9** | You comfortably mentor others in exhbiting this characteristic |
| **10** | You are the ideal example of this characteristic |

Now that you have completed your seven days of *power* development, let's take a snapshot of your knowledge level. After you assess your current level of knowledge per the matrix above, look back at your Day-Zero level of *power* knowledge. We would expect that your level has increased due to your developmental actions.

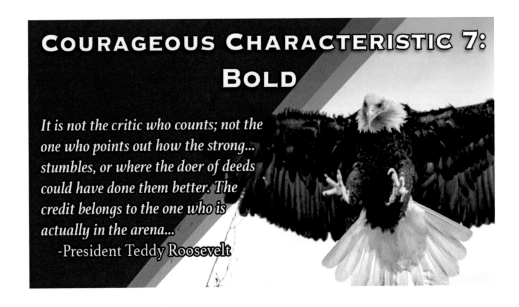

# COURAGEOUS CHARACTERISTIC 7: BOLD

*It is not the critic who counts; not the one who points out how the strong... stumbles, or where the doer of deeds could have done them better. The credit belongs to the one who is actually in the arena...*
-President Teddy Roosevelt

## *I am a Courageous Leader, therefore I am Bold!*

*Courageous Leadership* requires that you regularly step out of your comfort zone and take bold action. Not by exception but as the rule! Of course, you will be criticized for what others will call arrogance. Of course, you will be questioned for what others will call haste. But you will be the one boldly striving in the arena – thus your critics' comments will be muted by your successes.

Acting boldly is done with informed risk taking. We have discussed previously that leaders must decide without complete information. In fact, all decisions require a leap of faith from the known into the unknown. Those of spiritual persuasions are comfortable with leaps of faith in their religion. Those of the analytical persuasions are comfortable with leaps of faith in their scientific conclusions. Courageous Leaders must be equally comfortable making bold decisions with informed leaps of faith. With sufficient data gathered, risk adequately understood, and a course of action selected, these decisions are then executed with bold enthusiasm. An OK action plan executed with boldness is infinitely better than a perfect plan that either never materializes due to paralysis through analysis or is timidly executed.

In recognition of their maximized value delivery through proper T•C•E Alignment, Courageous Leaders boldly delegate critical tasks to trusted associates. Obviously, delegating tasks introduces additional risk, but is nonetheless required in order to focus your limited time and energy on those actions that will deliver the most value. Concurrently then, bold leaders develop their teams and organizations to ensure they are adequately prepared and can be trusted to assume their required duties.

Bold *Courageous Leaders* envision a world that stretches beyond the boundaries of currently accepted limits – be they technological, process, or cultural. Related to the vision characteristic, this exhibition of boldness adds yet another dimension by pushing beyond currently understood expectations – into unplowed fields – with unknown consequences and outcomes.

Boldness is an emotional state of mind as much as it is a technical or cognitive knowledge, skill, or ability. It is a "sense of being" that you are not part of the herd and that you are willing to stand out – thereby accepting the ultimate spotlight that accompanies such boldness. It is an eager willingness to enter a room and immediately assume the lead of all who are there. It is the ability to accept the limitless responsibilities of leadership with a calm peacefulness that you are doing your best, and someone must lead.

Finally, in line with the ideal of stretching your actions beyond the known into the unknown, to exhibit ideal Courageous Boldness, you must select goals that frighten you! If your goals are comfortable, then you are not being bold. If your goals are predictable, then you are not being bold. Only when your goals are on the edge of achievability are you exhibiting the boldness that you and your team deserve.

Starting a business is relatively easy – get a few licenses; find someone within your existing network who needs what you can provide; agree upon a price; and start delivering value to them. However, sustaining a business beyond this initial success – and the single point of failure it represents – is quite challenging. My experience was no exception.

Within a few months of hanging my shingle, I was working full time, earning a healthy hourly rate for as many hours as I could work, and had amassed a small team of other employees who were also billing full time. However, as nice as that situation was, I quickly realized I needed to broaden my risk across multiple streams of simultaneous revenue. This lesson was brought screaming home one otherwise beautiful morning as I was about to take off from the Honolulu Airport after visiting a work site, headed to Washington, DC. As I boarded the plane, my phone rang, and it was my only customer on the line. As I informed him they were closing the door to the plane, he quickly told me my only contract was being cancelled and we could talk more once I returned. Click, Buzz… Are you kidding me!

For the next eight hours, I contemplated the steps necessary to dissolve my new company, terminate my small team of employees – some whom had sold their homes in other parts of the country to join my great adventure; and how I was going to find a job to pay my mortgage. When I landed for a layover in Los Angeles, I quickly called my customer back and he gave me the rest of the story. They were in fact cancelling my existing contract but had every intention of immediately renewing my work through another existing contract. A small detail he had unfortunately not shared with me during our earlier brief conversation!

With that near catastrophe behind me, I realized bold action was required to ensure it never happened again. In order to begin managing this risk, I first had a conversation with my sole customer to let them know that I was not going to be the person arriving for work each morning – and that, although competent, the person replacing me was not at the same level of expertise and experience. I was able to convince him of this course of action by letting him know that although I would not be doing the work, I was going to be closely supervising the work. Further, I let him know if we didn't make the change, I would likely have to go away entirely in order to broaden my risk base.

Through these bold action, and thousands of others since then, I am fortunate to have survived and thrived. However, had I acted timidly in the face of the present risks, it is very likely I would have succumbed to the inevitability of my single point of failure actually failing.

# Dr. Martin Luther King, Jr.

Most of us are familiar with the work of Dr. Martin Luther King, Jr. to seek racial equality in the United States. One of his many examples of boldness is King's "Letter from Birmingham Jail." In the early 1960s, Birmingham, Alabama was the most segregated city in the United States. King's Birmingham Campaign was therefore organized to bring attention to the efforts being made toward the city's integration. It was planned as a nonviolent movement composed of coordinated sit-ins and marches, organized by the Alabama Christian Movement for Human Rights and King's Southern Christian Leadership Conference. However, a local circuit court judge issued an injunction that banned the activities planned for the campaign. As reported in *The Tuscaloosa News:*

*"The temporary injunction bans every imaginable form of demonstrations including boycotting, trespassing, parading, picketing, sit-ins, kneel-ins, wade-ins, and the inciting or encouraging of such acts."*

King responded to the injunction in a statement:

*"We cannot in all good conscience obey such an injunction which is an unjust, undemocratic and an unconstitutional misuse of the legal process."*

Thus, King was arrested and found himself in the Birmingham Jail. The day of his arrest, a public statement known as

"A Call for Unity, written by eight prominent white clergymen from Alabama, was published as an open letter in the Birmingham Newspaper. The open letter read in part,

*"We recognize the natural impatience of people who feel that their hopes are slow in being realized. But we are convinced that these demonstrations are unwise and untimely."*

In response, King stated,

*"Frankly, I have never yet engaged in a direct-action movement that was 'well timed' according to the timetable of those who have not suffered unduly from the disease of segregation."*

King went on to say;

*"For years now, I have heard the word 'Wait!' It rings in the ear of every Negro with piercing familiarity. This 'Wait' has almost always meant 'Never.' We must come to see, with the distinguished jurist of yesterday that 'justice too long delayed is justice denied."*

Following King's example, any leader would do well to remain consistently bold, as his actions and his letter literally changed the world, for the campaign ultimately forced desegregation in Birmingham and paved the way for the Civil Rights Act of 1964.

# Boldness Developmental Action

**Developmental Purpose:**

The purpose of this seven-day *Boldness-Development Action Phase* is to:

- Better understand the need for boldness;
- Identify your current level of boldness;
- Compare that finding to where you could/should be; and
- Take courageous action to close the gap.

**Journaling**

Journal these 7 days with a focus on your observations of boldness in your day-to-day actions. As you journal, please take particular care to capture the emotions, surprises, and new insights you experience and gain.

As you journal, verbally identify the differences between your observed boldness and desired boldness so that you may begin closing the gaps.

**Semi-Structured Conversation:**

Have a semi-structured conversation with:

- Yourself,
- A leader you consider especially bold (preferably not your Mentor).

Prior to the conversations, observe your subject and document in your journal the boldness you see in their day-to-day actions.

At the beginning of the conversation, summarize the philosophy of Courageous Leadership and the boldness characteristic for the interviewee.

During the conversation, capture the findings in your journal. Please take special care to capture the emotions, surprises, and new insights you experience and gain. Questions for this conversation might include:

- How bold are you currently?
- How bold should you be to accomplish your goals & objectives?
- Where is the balance between boldness and foolishness?

- When you get a great bold idea, how do you evaluate it?
- What do you do to counter fear or uneasiness so that you can boldly complete your mission or goal?
- What is your secret to delegating the right task to the right person at the right time?

In your journal, verbally identify the differences between your observed boldness and desired boldness so that you may begin closing the gaps.

**A.I.R. Hot Wash:**
Schedule a conversation with your Mentor to discuss A.I.R.
- **Advice**: What advice does he/she have for you regarding boldness in general – and specifically your level of boldness.
- **Information**: Ask your Mentor for sources of additional information that they have found useful regarding boldness.
- **Referrals**: Ask who you should speak to further about boldness.

In your journal, verbally identify the differences between your observed boldness and desired boldness so that you may begin closing the gaps.

**Bold Culminating Actions**: Given the identified gap between your current boldness and desired boldness:
- Include *Courageous Boldness Development* in your IDP. Identify developmental goals and activities. Developmental activities may include training (classroom, on-line, webinar), mentoring (either being a mentor or protégé), college courses, books (including audiobooks), developmental projects, stretch assignments, job shadowing, job rotation, networking opportunities, conferences, etc.
- Review and, if needed, modify your draft IMS to match your current understanding of boldness.
- Adjust your life and calendar accordingly to achieve this desired Courageous Boldness so that you may fulfill your IMS.
- Review and update as needed your W•F•S Balance & T•C•E Alignment.

**7-Day Summary:**

During this seven-day *Boldness Development Action Phase*, you have:

- Conducted in-depth self-reflection;
- Held semi-structured conversations with a "bold" leader;
- Sought advice, information, & referrals from your Mentor;
- Captured your emotions, surprises, and new insights from these 7 days of development in your journal;
- Measured your current level of boldness;
- Identified actions to achieve Courageous Boldness;
- Taken the initial steps to achieve Courageous Boldness; and
- Updated (as needed) your IMS, IDP, W•F•S Balance, & T•C•E Alignment.

**Bottom Line Value Creation:**

- With your strengthened appreciation for Courageous Boldness, you are prepared to make informed decisions and take action.

For each characteristic below, select the descriptor score that best matches your current knowledge level

| CHARACTERISTIC | SCORE 0-10 |
|---|---|
| **Principled** | |
| **TCE** | |
| **WFS** | |
| **Vision** | |
| **Humility** | |
| **Powerful** | |
| **Bold** | |
| **Driven** | |
| **Charismatic** | |
| **Unreasonable** | |
| **Total Score:** | |

| SCORE | DESCRIPTORS |
|---|---|
| 0 | You are unaware of this characteristic as a value-added part of leadership |
| 1 | You have just learned about this characteristic |
| 2 | You know about this characteristic but do not yet understand its value to your leadership |
| 3 | You understand the value of this characteristic but are not yet prepared to purposefully exhibit it |
| 4 | You understand the value of this characteristic and uneasily try to exhibit it when you remember |
| 5 | You understand the value of this characteristic and comfortably exhibit it when you remember |
| 6 | You comfortably exhibit this characteristic on almost all occasions |
| 7 | You recognize the growth of this characteristic in yourself and are naturally and confidently exhibiting it as a central part of your leadership |
| 8 | You are recognized by others for this characteristic as a particular strength |
| 9 | You comfortably mentor others in exhbiting this characteristic |
| 10 | You are the ideal example of this characteristic |

Now that you have completed your seven days of *boldness* development, let's take a snapshot of your knowledge level. After you assess your current level of knowledge per the matrix above, look back at your Day-Zero level of *boldness* knowledge. We would expect that your level has increased due to your developmental actions.

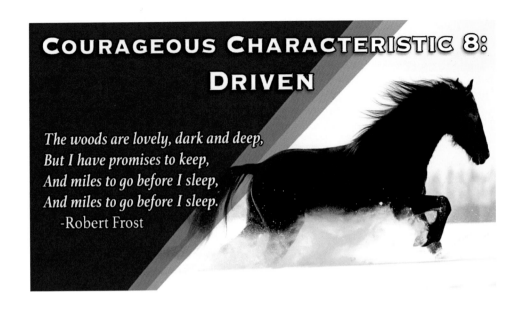

## COURAGEOUS CHARACTERISTIC 8:
## DRIVEN

*The woods are lovely, dark and deep,*
*But I have promises to keep,*
*And miles to go before I sleep,*
*And miles to go before I sleep.*
   -Robert Frost

# *I am a Courageous Leader, therefore I am Driven!*

We are about as smart as we are going to be the day we are born. We can gain knowledge and wisdom over time and experience, but the synapses are popping at their maximum speed when we emerge from the womb. Of course, some people are born smarter than others – they can solve problems easier; they can memorize better; they can learn languages quicker; and/or their IQs qualify them for Mensa. But that smartness will not provide break-out value unless it is accompanied with a sufficient level of drive.

Drive is what most-often separates the excellent from the average. Average levels of action will give you, at best, average results. Those of us who are born with normal levels of smartness can make up for our less-than-Mensa IQs with higher levels of drive. It is logical then to assume that if you want to achieve above-average outcomes, you must contribute above-average inputs. But to achieve "Break-Out" outcomes that are worthy of your life-long commitment to *Courageous Leadership*, you must contribute sustained inputs that are consistently multiple times greater than merely the average – i.e. you must be driven!

*Courageous Leaders* possess a self-motivated drive that compels them to achieve. I say self-motivated because no other person can make you driven. You can be motivated to perform as a follower through external uses of power such as rewards or coercion, but no amount of external motivation will make you courageously driven to achieve break-out leadership success. You must internalize the need to dedicate the necessary time and energy to achieve break-out success. Your internal willingness can be ignited through means such as self-reflection and mentoring, but you must ultimately accept the need for drive and personally commit to the ideal of demonstrating that drive through sustained action.

Just as the absence of courage is not cowardice, the absence of drive is not a negative – rather, it is normalcy. Normal people do not have trouble sleeping because they are brainstorming the third-level effects of their five-year strategic plan; normal people do not initiate action today in fulfillment of a vision 30-years in the future.

Drive can be both a blessing and a curse – if you allow it. The blessings will be obvious in your achievements. The curse can come from drive that is not tempered with W•F•S Balance. Achieving "success" to the detriment of family, friends, or personal health is not actually success! If you get to the finish line alone and/or an invalid, then you have not won!

In order to fulfill their innate desires to achieve, driven people often find themselves leading. As they craft their visions, create plans to fulfill those visions, and communicate those visions to associates, friends, and loved ones, driven people often find themselves surrounded by others willing to follow their visions. Likewise, as they burn to achieve, driven people often feel compelled to gather smart, capable people who can assist them in achieving.

In order to maximize their value contributions, driven leaders must ensure they are dedicating their sustained time and energy to those actions that will create the greatest outputs. Thus, they must continually align their T•C•E intelligence to ensure they are optimizing their opportunity costs.

During a particularly challenging time in my business, I was driving to work one morning after an overnight snow fall. As often happens in Virginia, the snow was already melting in the early morning light under the steady down pour of a freezing rain. Thus, the ground was covered with a thick layer of icy cold slush. The added danger and blustery conditions only further exacerbated my foul mood as I was driving toward yet another challenging day.

As I eased my car toward the stop sign at the end of our housing development, I spotted two vultures eating a dead animal. As I inched closer, I realized their breakfast was a dead skunk. The one on the right was observing his companion who had a mouth full of the dead skunk's rear end. As I eased to a stop, staring intently at the pair, he looked at me with an indignant gaze – that strongly suggested *"What are you staring at?"*

When I came to my senses a few seconds later, and finally made the right turn toward work, my challenges seemed suddenly diminished – for, even though they were daunting, at least I wasn't six inches deep in ice-cold slush, under a freezing rain, eating the rear-end out of a dead skunk! So, I picked my head up and drove on – both literally behind the wheel of my car and figuratively as the leader of my company and family.

## Thomas Edison

One has to look no further than Thomas Edison to observe life-long drive in demonstrated successful action. Through his unrelenting hard work – he did not accept the title of genius – Edison brought us every day items such as the copy machine; the movie camera; and the phonograph. Over the course of his life, Edison submitted 2332 patents for review and was successfully granted 1,903. In other words, over the course of his life, Edison invented nearly 2,000 things that did not previously exist – with his first patent awarded at age 21 and last at age 84. Examine just that fact alone and you can easily see what a driven life he led – with an average of nearly 40 inventions per year.

Like many similarly successful people, Edison used his drive to overcome other challenges in his life – such as being labeled as "troubled" and "stupid" in his youth. As the youngest of seven children, Edison possessed only 12 weeks of formal elementary school education, as his teachers refused to instruct him due to his unruly behavior in class. Also, Edison was nearly deaf throughout his entire life due to a battle with scarlet fever.

When reflecting upon his most famous work – developing the first commercially viable incandescent light bulb – you see the dogged drive in its clearest format. Edison unsuccessfully tested over 1,000 versions of the bulb before his first successful test. One can only imagine the frustration with his 1st bulb failure; and then his 100th; and then his 1000th!

All the while, Edison was confronted with the same challenges we face in our own lives – children to feed at home; equipment and space to pay for; and life's day-to-day distractions tugging at his resolve. And his other successful inventions experienced similar trial and error over many years as he worked to prefect the technologies.

# Driven Developmental Action

**Developmental Purpose:**

The purpose of the seven-day *Drive-Developmental Action Phase* is to:

- Better understand drive;
- Identify your current level of drive;
- Compare that finding to where you could/should be; and
- Take courageous action to close the gap.

**Journaling**

Journal these 7 days with a focus on your observations of drive in your day-to-day actions. As you journal, please take particular care to capture the emotions, surprises, and new insights you experience and gain.

As you journal, verbally identify the differences between your observed drive and desired drive so that you may begin closing the gaps.

**Semi-Structured Conversation:**

Have a semi-structured conversation with:

- Yourself,
- A leader you consider especially driven (preferably not your Mentor).

Prior to the interview, observe your subjects and document in your journal the drive you see in their day-to-day actions.

At the beginning of the conversations, summarize the philosophy of Courageous Leadership and drive for the interviewee.

During the conversations, capture the findings in your journal. Questions for these conversations might include:

- How driven are you currently? Do they consider themselves particularly driven?
- How driven should you be to accomplish your goals & objectives?
- What 2-3 things you must start doing and 2-3 things you must stop doing to live a driven life?
- How do they manage their drive and W•F•S Balance?

In your journal, verbally identify the differences between your observed drive and desired drive so that you may begin closing the gaps.

**A.I.R. Hot Wash:**

Schedule a conversation with your Mentor to discuss A.I.R.

- **Advice**: What advice does he/she have for you regarding drive in general – and specifically your level of drive.
- **Information**: Ask your Mentor for sources of additional information that they have found useful regarding drive.
- **Referrals**: Ask who you should speak to further about drive.

In your journal, verbally identify the differences between your observed drive and desired drive so that you may begin closing the gaps.

**Drive Culminating Actions**: Given the identified gap between your current drive and desired drive:

- Include *Courageous Drive Development* in your IDP. Identify developmental goals and activities. Developmental activities may include training (classroom, on-line, webinar), mentoring (either being a mentor or protégé), college courses, books (including audiobooks), developmental projects, stretch assignments, job shadowing, job rotation, networking opportunities, conferences, etc.
- Review and, if needed, modify your draft IMS to match your current understanding of drive.
- Adjust your life and calendar accordingly to achieve this desired Courageous Drive so that you may fulfill your IMS.
- Review and update as needed your W•F•S Balance & T•C•E Alignment.

**7-Day Summary:**

During this seven-day *Drive Development Action Phase*, you have:

- Conducted in-depth self-reflection;
- Held a semi-structured conversation with a "driven" leader;
- Sought advice, information, & referrals from your Mentor;
- Captured your emotions, surprises, and new insights from these 7 days of development in your journal;
- Measured your current level of drive;
- Identified actions to achieve Courageous Drive;
- Taken the initial steps to achieve Courageous Drive; and
- Updated (as needed) your IMS, IDP, W•F•S Balance, & T•C•E Alignment.

**Bottom Line Value Creation:**

- Given your recognition that sustained drive, balanced with WFS, is often the difference between average and excellent, you are prepared to excel.

For each characteristic below, select the descriptor score that best matches your current knowledge level

| Characteristic | Score 0-10 |
|---|---|
| **Principled** | |
| **TCE** | |
| **WFS** | |
| **Vision** | |
| **Humility** | |
| **Powerful** | |
| **Bold** | |
| **Driven** | |
| **Charismatic** | |
| **Unreasonable** | |
| **Total Score:** | |

| Score | Descriptors |
|---|---|
| 0 | You are unaware of this characteristic as a value-added part of leadership |
| 1 | You have just learned about this characteristic |
| 2 | You know about this characteristic but do not yet understand its value to your leadership |
| 3 | You understand the value of this characteristic but are not yet prepared to purposefully exhibit it |
| 4 | You understand the value of this characteristic and uneasily try to exhibit it when you remember |
| 5 | You understand the value of this characteristic and comfortably exhibit it when you remember |
| 6 | You comfortably exhibit this characteristic on almost all occasions |
| 7 | You recognize the growth of this characteristic in yourself and are naturally and confidently exhibiting it as a central part of your leadership |
| 8 | You are recognized by others for this characteristic as a particular strength |
| 9 | You comfortably mentor others in exhbiting this characteristic |
| 10 | You are the ideal example of this characteristic |

Now that you have completed your seven days of *drive* development, let's take a snapshot of your knowledge level. After you assess your current level of knowledge per the matrix above, look back at your Day-Zero level of *drive* knowledge. We would expect that your level has increased due to your developmental actions.

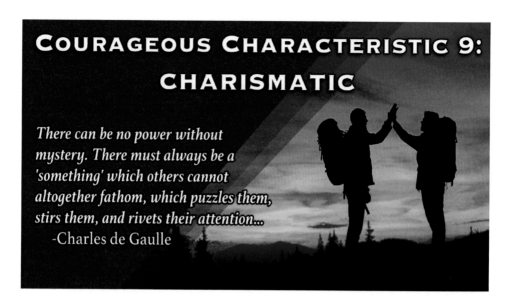

# COURAGEOUS CHARACTERISTIC 9: CHARISMATIC

*There can be no power without mystery. There must always be a 'something' which others cannot altogether fathom, which puzzles them, stirs them, and rivets their attention...*
   -Charles de Gaulle

## *I am a Courageous Leader, therefore I am Charismatic!*

Charisma is defined by the English Oxford dictionary as:

*"...a compelling attractiveness that inspires devotion in others..."*

Teams and organizations want and need *Courageous Charismatic Leadership*. Throughout time, we human beings have painted images on cave walls, told stories about, and written about such memorable leaders. This kind of *"compelling attractiveness"* can and should be purposefully developed as another significant arrow in your *Courageous Leadership* quiver.

Storytelling is an excellent and even necessary technique through which to demonstrate your *Courageous Leadership* while increasing your charismatic appeal. What are your principles? Tell that story! How important is W•F•S Balance to you? Tell that story! What is your vision? Tell that story - again, and again, and again! Tell your stories with simultaneous humility and boldness! And tell stories about others within and external to your teams and organizations that you desire your teams and organizations emulate.

Your willingness & ability to be charismatic is demonstrated over time through the collective value you produce by living through the *Courageous Leadership Characteristics*. Thus, charisma is developed and sustained quite naturally by courageously leading your teams and organizations. Through exhibiting the characteristics of *Courageous Leadership,* others will begin to recognize this *"compelling attractiveness"* in you as a natural byproduct of the value they realize from your leadership actions.

Ultimately, charisma is the unspoken recognition of your demonstrated admiration and respect – even love – for the individual members of your teams and organizations! When charisma is seemingly immediate, as is often the case with movie stars and politicians, it is the *hope* for this admiration and respect the giver projects onto the charismatic recipient. However, when charisma is genuinely created and sustained over time, it is the *fulfillment of that hope* through your delivery of admiration and respect (love) as a *Courageous Leader*! Over time, as your power shifts from positional to referent, charisma will be central to the admiration and respect your teams and organizations will naturally associate to you and your leadership.

Your admiration and respect – even love – for the individual members of your teams and organizations can be easily demonstrated through your expressed genuine interest and concern for their well-being. Do you know their names and the names of their children? Do you know their hopes and dreams? And do they know you support the fulfillment of their hopes and dreams? Show them and tell them -- again and again!

Your challenge is to recognize charisma's legitimacy, accept the role, and purposefully leverage this charismatic characteristic with the same vigor with which you accept your other *Courageous Leadership* responsibilities. You, your teams, and your organizations deserve nothing less.

The eighth grade for me was the apex of my personal rebellion against all things school and authority related. So, imagine my disgust and shock when I was assigned to a U.S. History Course with "*The Major.*" This particular gentleman was infamous amongst my crowd of slackers for his reputation as a harsh grader, a strict disciplinarian, and an authoritarian. He was a Major in the U.S. Army Reserves. So, I walked into the room on the first day of class full of disdain; slouched into the back row; and immediately decided I would learn nothing in the coming 12 weeks.

That day was over 40 years ago! He is now well into his eighties. And I have visited him regularly while home visiting family – as recently as three years ago. For during those 12 weeks, he lit a spark in me – with nothing more than his daily examples of how he and others had overcome their personal challenges –a spark that has burned brightly ever since.

Slowly but surely his personal confidence; along with his eccentric teaching style; and countless stories that had nothing to do with U.S. History; created an aura of charisma that has resonated so strongly with me that I have wanted to make him proud of me every day since.

# Aung San Suu Kyi

6

Aung San Suu Kyi, a textbook example of charisma in action, was born in Yangon, Myanmar (formerly Burma), in 1945. Her father, Aung San, was Commander of the Burma Independence Army and helped negotiate Burma's independence from Britain. He was assassinated on July 19, 1947, when Suu Kyi was two years old.

Myanmar was ruled by the Burma Socialist Programme Party headed by its military leader, General Ne Win, as a one-party state since it took power in a military coup in 1962. His "Burmese Way to Socialism" had driven the country into abject poverty. By the late 1980s, protests and demonstrations were taking place against his government – which he suppressed with extreme violence – the largest of which was held on August 8, 1988.

In September of 1988, General Ne Win was driven from power, but a new military junta immediately seized power. These actions prompted Suu Kyi to start the National League for Democracy (NLD), a party dedicated to nonviolence and civil

---

disobedience. Soon after starting the NLD, she was placed under house arrest under charges of trying to divide the military. She was concurrently given permission to leave Burma under the condition that she never return. But Suu Kyi chose to stay with the people she had been struggling with and for. In making this decision to stay, she knowingly gave up a life with her two young sons and her husband – to remain in service to her followers. From 1989 to 2010, Suu Kyi was under house arrest for fifteen of the twenty-one years. Throughout this time, her resolve, sacrifice, and leadership created an unbreakable bond with her compatriots.

And her popularity only continued to grow – and with it her power. In 1991, Suu Kyi was awarded the Sakharov Prize for Freedom of Thought from the European Parliament and the Nobel Peace Prize for her "non-violent struggle for democracy and human rights." Both of which only further increased her popularity and power.

Suu Kyi was finally released from house arrest in 2010. Even then, she immediately pledged to the NLD, in front of the world press, to continue working for the restoration of democracy and human rights in Myanmar. In 2015, her life's work finally came to realization as the NLD won a landslide victory, giving them a majority control of the Myanmar Parliament.

We are all well-served to strive for such ideals of charismatic leadership!

# Charisma Developmental Action

**Developmental Purpose:**

The purpose of this seven-day *Charisma-Development Action Phase* is to:

- Better understand charisma;
- Identify your current level of charisma;
- Compare that finding to where you could/should be; and
- Take courageous action to close the gap.

**Journaling**

Journal these 7 days with a focus on your observations of charisma in your day-to-day actions. As you journal, please take particular care to capture the emotions, surprises, and new insights you experience and gain.

As you journal, verbally identify the differences between your observed charisma and desired charisma so that you may begin closing the gaps.

**Semi-Structured Conversation:**

Have a semi-structured conversation with:

- Yourself,
- A leader you consider especially charismatic (preferably not your Mentor).

Prior to the interview, observe your subjects and document in your journal how charismatic you see them in their day-to-day actions.

At the beginning of the conversations, summarize the philosophy of Courageous Leadership and charisma for the interviewee.

During the conversations, capture the findings in your journal. Questions for these conversations might include:

- How charismatic are you currently? Do you consider yourself charismatic?
- How charismatic should you be to accomplish your goals & objectives?
- What purposeful actions do they take to strengthen their charisma?

- Describe a leader you know who is charismatic. What actions, behaviors or attitudes reflect their charisma?
- What steps have you taken to show the people on your team how much you appreciate and respect them?
- Do you show genuine interest and concern for every person on your team? Do you know the names of their children? Do you know their hopes and dreams? Do they know you support the fulfillment of their hopes and dreams?

In your journal, verbally identify the differences between your observed charisma and desired charisma so that you may begin closing the gaps.

**A.I.R. Hot Wash:**

Schedule a conversation with your Mentor to discuss A.I.R.
- **Advice**: What advice does he/she have for you regarding charisma in general – and specifically your level of charisma.
- **Information**: Ask your Mentor for sources of additional information that they have found useful regarding charisma.
- **Referrals**: Ask who you should speak to further about charisma.

In your journal, verbally identify the differences between your observed charisma and desired charisma so that you may begin closing the gaps.

**Charisma Culminating Actions**: Given the identified gap between your current charisma and desired charisma:
- Include *Courageous Charisma Development* in your IDP. Identify developmental goals and activities. Developmental activities may include training (classroom, on-line, webinar), mentoring (either being a mentor or protégé), college courses, books (including audiobooks), developmental projects, stretch assignments, job shadowing, job rotation, networking opportunities, conferences, etc.
- Review and, if needed, modify your draft IMS to match your current understanding of charisma.
- Adjust your life and calendar accordingly to achieve this desired Courageous Charisma so that you may fulfill your IMS.

- Review and update as needed your W•F•S Balance & T•C•E Alignment.

**7-Day Summary:**
During this seven-day *Charisma Development* action phase, you have:
- Conducted in-depth self-reflection;
- Held a semi-structured conversation with a "charismatic" leader;
- Sought advice, information, & referrals from your Mentor;
- Captured your emotions, surprises, and new insights from these 7 days of development in your journal;
- Measured your current level of charisma;
- Identified actions to achieve Courageous Charisma;
- Taken the initial steps to achieve Courageous Charisma; and
- Updated (as needed_ your IMS, IDP, W•F•S Balance, & T•C•E Alignment.

**Bottom Line Value Creation:**
- Given your recognition of charisma's invaluable role in building culture and commitment, you have accepted the role & responsibility of creating, collecting, and using Courageous Charisma in your leadership roles.

For each characteristic below, select the descriptor score that best matches your current knowledge level

| CHARACTERISTIC | SCORE 0-10 |
|---|---|
| **Principled** | |
| **TCE** | |
| **WFS** | |
| **Vision** | |
| **Humility** | |
| **Powerful** | |
| **Bold** | |
| **Driven** | |
| **Charismatic** | |
| **Unreasonable** | |
| **Total Score:** | |

| SCORE | DESCRIPTORS |
|---|---|
| 0 | You are unaware of this characteristic as a value-added part of leadership |
| 1 | You have just learned about this characteristic |
| 2 | You know about this characteristic but do not yet understand its value to your leadership |
| 3 | You understand the value of this characteristic but are not yet prepared to purposefully exhibit it |
| 4 | You understand the value of this characteristic and uneasily try to exhibit it when you remember |
| 5 | You understand the value of this characteristic and comfortably exhibit it when you remember |
| 6 | You comfortably exhibit this characteristic on almost all occasions |
| 7 | You recognize the growth of this characteristic in yourself and are naturally and confidently exhibiting it as a central part of your leadership |
| 8 | You are recognized by others for this characteristic as a particular strength |
| 9 | You comfortably mentor others in exhbiting this characteristic |
| 10 | You are the ideal example of this characteristic |

Now that you have completed your seven days of *charisma* development, let's take a snapshot of your knowledge level. After you assess your current level of knowledge per the matrix above, look back at your Day-Zero level of *charisma* knowledge. We would expect that your level has increased due to your developmental actions.

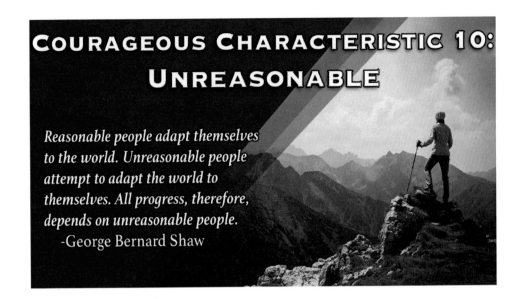

# COURAGEOUS CHARACTERISTIC 10: UNREASONABLE

*Reasonable people adapt themselves to the world. Unreasonable people attempt to adapt the world to themselves. All progress, therefore, depends on unreasonable people.*
-George Bernard Shaw

## *I am a Courageous Leader, therefore I am Unreasonable!*

With *Principled* as the foundational courageous characteristic, *Unreasonable* is the culminating – as all other characteristics play a role in executing it.  To be principled is often considered unreasonable; to align T•C•E and balance W•F•S – unreasonable; to live visionary, humble, powerful, bold, driven, and charismatic lives – unreasonable.  Embrace it! Cherish it!  For you have chosen, in your pursuit of *Courageous Leadership*, to live a life of exception!

Navy SEALS calculate that the average person becomes "exhausted" at just 40% of their body's actual capacity.  Knowing this, they "unreasonably" expect themselves and especially their SEAL candidates to perform far beyond the "reasonable" levels of exhaustion.  Your understanding of this fact presents the possibility of significantly greater performance – if you are simply willing to be regularly unreasonable.  Of course, one must be careful, for these levels of performance are unsustainable over time and 100% exhaustion equals death!

If you can think of past industry disruptions, the visionary leader who provided the catalyst for change was almost always considered unreasonable! Ford – unreasonable; Bezos – unreasonable; Musk -- unreasonable! Even further back in history, can you imagine the first person who chose to milk a cow? The sequence of events went something like this:

1) Unreasonable Person: *I am so hungry, I am going to chase down this beast and steal the food from its baby*;
2) Reasonable Person: *That's crazy, sit down and eat your berries!*
3) Unreasonable Person: *But we are all starving – there are not enough berries*;
4) Reasonable Person: *That's crazy, don't rock the rock!*
5) Unreasonable Person: *I don't care what you say – I am going for it!*
6) Reasonable Person: *Man, that tastes good – let's do it again!*

And so the story goes for every change in the history of the world! Socrates was executed for asking probing questions; Copernicus was nearly executed when he informed the world the sun was at the center of the universe; you will be questioned for unreasonably introducing new realms of the possible.

Per Einstein's definition of insanity, unreasonable *Courageous Leaders* recognize that change comes only from doing things differently. The primary component of vision is to identify a different reality at some point in the future and begin its creation. Doing so, by definition, requires you to unreasonably break from currently accepted routines.

In execution of your courageous power for unreasonable change, you must expect and demand that the world bend to your will. While being regularly unreasonable, the courageous leader accepts the inherent criticism that comes from *"coloring outside the lines."*

While I was serving as a Drill Instructor, I applied for and was accepted into a year-long college preparatory school – which if I completed successfully, would lead to acceptance into a college-degree program – and eventually my commissioning as an Officer. The curriculum for the 12 months was a high school refresher designed to get us ready for our freshman year in college. However, if you didn't initially learn the subjects in high school, the material was all new.

As the enthusiastic new guy, I visited the training center two weeks early just to introduce myself. The experience was not encouraging. The senior person there looked up from his desk and said:

*"With all due respect, I wouldn't unpack your bags when you get here because you're only going to be here about two weeks and you're going to go right back to life as an enlisted Marine. I've read your transcripts, I've read your bio, and you're just not going to make it..."*

To his credit, the course did experience a 60% attrition rate throughout its history. True to the words of caution I had received, the curriculum was indeed a butt-kicker for me. Despite working twenty-hour days, I found myself on the precipice of failure every week. Even after moving out of my home to avoid the 40-mile commute; leaving my new wife and even newer son; and taking up residence in the school building; I still struggled mightily – each day just one more failed test away from returning to my enlisted career. To this day, those 12 months were the most mentally and physically challenging of my life!

But I persevered – scraping by week after week just above the cut line! To my surprise, at the graduation party a few days before the year ended, I learned the entire school had a betting pool guessing the day and month that I would finally fail and be sent packing. Ironically, the next day, I was asked to speak to the incoming class to explain how I had survived.

My message was clear and simple! Early on in the year, I had decided to be entirely unreasonable and not allow myself to fail! When 20-hour days five days a week proved insufficient, I unreasonably increased the pace to 20-hour days seven days a week; when group night study sessions every evening proved insufficient, then I unreasonably sought one-on-one tutoring every evening after the group night study sessions; when 20-hour days and one-on-one tutoring proved insufficient, then I unreasonably sought additional instruction during my lunch hours with the professors. My objective was clear – succeed or die!

Thus, across the intervening years, I have grown completely comfortable being completely unreasonable!

# Jeff Bezos

7

Jeff Bezos, founder of Amazon.com, is the poster child for Unreasonable Courage. Not only did he unreasonably leave a lucrative position at a successful hedge fund to start a new business, but he started a business that changed the entire paradigm of how we purchase – at first books – but now almost everything. Can you imagine the conversations Bezos had with anyone and everyone when he pitched the idea for Amazon's business model – to his wife; to potential investors; to his previous employer? To a person, they must have all said, in one form or another – "Can't you be just a bit less unreasonable in your expectations?"

Beyond the initial bout of unreasonableness that started Amazon, Bezos has a long track record of unreasonable tendencies – such as his maxim that, "No team should be so large that it cannot be fed with just two pizzas." Bezos acknowledges that big teams are necessary to make big strides, but says they need to be "subdivided." His idea is that "humans grew up around campfires and telling each other stories" and that social groups tend to cluster in 10s and 12s. He told *GeekWire*, "That's the perfect size to have natural human coordination without a lot of structure." Further, Bezos demands that his teams embrace failure, for he unreasonably believes that, "failure and invention are inseparable twins." In a 2014 interview

7 By James Duncan Davidson from Portland, USA - Etech05: Jeff, CC BY 2.0, https://commons.wikimedia.org/w/index.php?curid=2576474

with Business Insider, Bezos expounded, "Experiments are, by their very nature, prone to failure. A few big successes compensate for dozens and dozens of things that didn't work. Bold bets - Amazon Web Services, Kindle, Amazon Prime, and our third-party seller business - all of those things are examples of bold bets that did work, and they pay for a lot of experiments." It looks easy to say, standing at the helm of what is poised to become a trillion-dollar company, but Bezos continues, "I've made billions of dollars of failures at Amazon.com. Literally billions of dollars of failures. You might remember Pets.com or Kosmo.com. It was like getting a root canal with no anesthesia."

We should all be so lucky as to be so unreasonable!

# Unreasonable Developmental Action

**Developmental Purpose:**

The purpose of this seven-day *Unreasonable-Development Action Phase* is to:

- Better understand unreasonableness;
- Identify your current level of unreasonableness;
- Compare that finding to where you could/should be; and
- Take courageous action to close the gap.

**Journaling**

Journal these 7 days with a focus on your observations of unreasonableness in your W•F•S. As you journal, please take particular care to capture the emotions, surprises, and new insights you experience and gain. Specific focus areas might include:

- How unreasonable are you currently?
- How unreasonable should you be to accomplish your goals & objectives?

As you journal, verbally identify the differences between your observed unreasonableness and desired unreasonableness so that you may begin closing the gaps.

**Semi-Structured Conversation:**

Identify someone in your W•F•S sphere you consider unreasonable per the definition we have put forth in this book (preferably not your Mentor). Journal their behaviors. Identify what characteristics they display that make them unreasonable. Map their unreasonable characteristics as T, C, or E? Conduct a semi-structured conversation with them. Topics of discussion might include:

- Do they consider themselves unreasonable?
- What purposeful actions do they take to strengthen their unreasonable behaviors?

In your journal, verbally identify the differences between your observed unreasonableness and desired unreasonableness so that you may begin closing the gaps.

**A.I.R. Hot Wash:**

Schedule a conversation with your Mentor to discuss A.I.R.

- **Advice**: What advice does he/she have for you regarding being unreasonable in general – and specifically your level of unreasonableness.
- **Information**: Ask your Mentor for sources of additional information that they have found useful regarding being unreasonable.
- **Referrals**: Ask who you should speak to further about being unreasonable.

In your journal, verbally identify the differences between your observed unreasonableness and desired unreasonableness so that you may begin closing the gaps.

**Culminating Actions**: Given the identified gap between your current unreasonableness and desired unreasonableness:

- Include *Courageous Unreasonableness Development* in your IDP. Identify developmental goals and activities. Developmental activities may include training (classroom, on-line, webinar), mentoring (either being a mentor or protégé), college courses, books (including audiobooks), developmental projects, stretch assignments, job shadowing, job rotation, networking opportunities, conferences, etc.
- Review and, if needed, modify your draft IMS to match your current understanding of being unreasonable.
- Adjust your life and calendar accordingly to achieve this desired Courageous Unreasonableness so that you may fulfill your IMS.
- Review and update as needed your W•F•S Balance & T•C•E Alignment.

**7-Day Summary:**

During this seven-day *Unreasonableness Development* phase, you have:

- Conducted in-depth self-reflection;
- Held a semi-structured conversation with an "unreasonable" leader;
- Captured your emotions, surprises, and new insights from these 7 days of development in your journal;
- Sought advice, information, & referrals from your Mentor;

- Measured your current level of unreasonableness;
- Identified actions to achieve Courageous Unreasonableness;
- Taken the initial steps to achieve that Courageous Unreasonableness; and
- Updated (as needed) your IMS, IDP, W•F•S Balance, & T•C•E Alignment.

**Bottom Line Value Creation:**
- Now understanding that all change comes from being positively unreasonable, you are prepared to move forward being completely comfortable being completely unreasonable.

For each characteristic below, select the descriptor score that best matches your current knowledge level

| Characteristic | Score 0-10 |
|---|---|
| **Principled** | |
| **TCE** | |
| **WFS** | |
| **Vision** | |
| **Humility** | |
| **Powerful** | |
| **Bold** | |
| **Driven** | |
| **Charismatic** | |
| **Unreasonable** | |
| **Total Score:** | |

| Score | Descriptors |
|---|---|
| **0** | You are unaware of this characteristic as a value-added part of leadership |
| **1** | You have just learned about this characteristic |
| **2** | You know about this characteristic but do not yet understand its value to your leadership |
| **3** | You understand the value of this characteristic but are not yet prepared to purposefully exhibit it |
| **4** | You understand the value of this characteristic and uneasily try to exhibit it when you remember |
| **5** | You understand the value of this characteristic and comfortably exhibit it when you remember |
| **6** | You comfortably exhibit this characteristic on almost all occasions |
| **7** | You recognize the growth of this characteristic in yourself and are naturally and confidently exhibiting it as a central part of your leadership |
| **8** | You are recognized by others for this characteristic as a particular strength |
| **9** | You comfortably mentor others in exhbiting this characteristic |
| **10** | You are the ideal example of this characteristic |

Now that you have completed your seven days of *unreasonable* development, let's take a snapshot of your knowledge level. After you assess your current level of knowledge per the matrix above, look back at your Day-Zero level of *unreasonable* knowledge. We would expect that your level has increased due to your developmental actions.

131

# CHAPTER 5:
## A LIFE-LONG PATH TOWARD MASTERY

*The journey of a thousand miles begins with one step.*
-Lao Tzu

Lao Tzu, recognized as the father of Taoism, correctly captures your requirement to now begin your life-long path to mastering Courageous Leadership with a single step. And then another. And another. For the remainder of your life. For this noble and worthy pursuit will fill the remainder of your life.

# A Life-Long Path Toward Mastery

**Developmental Outcomes:**

During these twelve weeks, through completing the developmental actions listed below, you achieved a level of "proficiency" with each of the ten *Courageous Leadership* characteristics – which will now serve as the baseline for your further leadership development.

Concurrently, and perhaps even more importantly, you either drafted for the first time or further clarified and then began executing your lifetime goals & objectives. This second outcome is especially critical in that it provides the tangible products upon which you will leverage your new-found leadership abilities.

- 12 weeks of Journaling
- 28 Semi-Structured Conversations
- 12 Mentor/Protégé A.I.R. Hot Washes
- 1 Draft Individual Mission Statement (IMS)
- 11 IMS Reviews
- 1 Draft Individual Development Plan (IDP)
- 12 IDP Reviews
- 1 Draft Lifetime Goals & Objectives (LG&O)
- 1 Revised LG&O
- 16 New or Strengthened Relationships
- 10 Courageous Leadership Characteristics Gap Analyses
- 1 T•C•E Alignment
- 10 T•C•E Alignment Reviews
- 1 W•F•S Balance
- 9 W•F•S Balance Reviews
- 12 Courageous Leadership Characteristics Measurements

With this mountain of work behind you, it is now time to clearly identify your next steps so that you may build upon the proficiency you have gained; continue developing your courageous characteristics; achieve your lifetime goals & objectives; and ultimately pass along your knowledge, skills, abilities, & experiences to the next generation of Courageous Leaders.

You should sustain your investment in your developmental tools – to include daily Journaling, focused Semi-Structured Conversations, and regular Mentor/Protégé Hot Washes. Likewise, you should continue capturing your developmental actions in iterative Courageous Characteristics Knowledge Measurements, Individual Development Plans, and Individual Mission Statements. Let's walk through what that continued investment will look like.

**1) Courageous Characteristics Knowledge Measurements (CCKM):** Now that you have completed your 12 weeks of Courageous Leadership developmental actions, let's take another snapshot of your knowledge level. We will use this snapshot to inform your next developmental actions. This matrix is available at

For each characteristic below, select the descriptor score that best matches your current knowledge level

| Characteristic | Score 0-10 |
|---|---|
| Principled | |
| TCE | |
| WFS | |
| Vision | |
| Humility | |
| Powerful | |
| Bold | |
| Driven | |
| Charismatic | |
| Unreasonable | |
| **Total Score:** | |

| Score | Descriptors |
|---|---|
| 0 | You are unaware of this characteristic as a value-added part of leadership |
| 1 | You have just learned about this characteristic |
| 2 | You know about this characteristic but do not yet understand its value to your leadership |
| 3 | You understand the value of this characteristic but are not yet prepared to purposefully exhibit it |
| 4 | You understand the value of this characteristic and uneasily try to exhibit it when you remember |
| 5 | You understand the value of this characteristic and comfortably exhibit it when you remember |
| 6 | You comfortably exhibit this characteristic on almost all occasions |
| 7 | You recognize the growth of this characteristic in yourself and are naturally and confidently exhibiting it as a central part of your leadership |
| 8 | You are recognized by others for this characteristic as a particular strength |
| 9 | You comfortably mentor others in exhbiting this characteristic |
| 10 | You are the ideal example of this characteristic |

*FLATTER LEADERSHIP*

www.FlatterLeadership.com/Assessment

**2) Individual Development Plan (IDP):** As you journaled; held your semi-structured conversations; measured your characteristics knowledge levels; and conducted your Mentor/Protégé A.I.R. meetings, you captured potential developmental activities in your Individual Development Plan (IDP). We will now use this collected information to inform you next developmental actions.

| CHARACTERISTIC | DEVELOPMENTAL ACTIVITY | COMMENTS |
|---|---|---|
| Principled | | |
| Technically, Cognitively & Emotionally Aligned | | |
| Work, Family, & Self Balanced | | |
| Visionary | | |
| Humble | | |
| Powerful | | |
| Bold | | |
| Driven | | |
| Charismatic | | |
| Unreasonable | | |

As a reminder, developmental actions may include training (classroom, on-line, webinar), mentoring (either being a mentor or protégé), college courses, books (including audio books), developmental projects, stretch assignments, job shadowing, job rotation, networking opportunities, conferences, etc.

**3) Individual Mission Statement (IMS):** And, as a regular part of your developmental actions over the past twelve weeks, you drafted and refined your Individual Mission Statement (IMS). We will now use this IMS to inform you next developmental actions.

| | |
|---|---|
| **Who am I?**<br>• I am a loving Spouse, Parent, Sibling, Friend, & Leader. | **In these roles, I am guided by:**<br>• My love for my Wife, Family, and Fellow Man;<br>• My commitment to continually educating myself and others; and<br>• My services as a Courageous Leader. |
| **What do I believe in?**<br>• The *Courageous Characteristics*<br>  • Principled<br>  • TCE Aligned<br>  • WFS Balanced<br>  • Visionary<br>  • Humble<br>  • Powerful<br>  • Bold<br>  • Driven<br>  • Charismatic<br>  • Unreasonable | **How do these beliefs guide my life?**<br>• I subscribe to the *Courageous Characteristics* to guide my life as I fulfill my leadership roles. |
| **What are my deepest passions?**<br>• I have a passion for leading and developing leaders. | **How do these passions impact my life?**<br>• My role as a father is primarily that of leader and leader developer;<br>• My role as a businessman is primarily that of leader and leader developer; and<br>• My role as a community servant is primarily that of leader and leader developer. |
| **What do I aspire to be?**<br>• I aspire to leave behind a vibrant company | **How do these aspirations influence my actions?**<br>• So that my family and team may continue to fulfill their life's goals & objectives. |

**4) Life Goals & Objectives (LG&O)**: Likewise, you have envisioned your Lifetime Goals & Objectives (LG&O). Let's now revise that draft document with the knowledge gained from our other developmental exercises. As a reminder, the template is broken into goals & objectives for 30-Years, 10-Year, 1-year, and Today. Further, we work backward from 30 years, as the farthest goals & objectives inform and enable the nearer ones. Remember, goals are abstract while objectives are tangible. Likewise, the farther in the future the less detail needed.

| Life-Goal 1: *Educate My Children* | | |
|---|---|---|
| **MILESTONE** | **GOAL** | **OBJECTIVES** |
| 30-Year | • Educate my Children at the world's finest universities | • Financing is in Place to Fund four degrees |
| 10-Year | • My Children are all High School Graduates with strong GPAs and varied extra-curricular activities | • All are accepted to universities of their choice |
| 1-Year | • My Children are on a path to becoming well-rounded students | • Spend time tutoring my Children<br>• Enroll them in extra-curricular activities |
| Today | • My children are in school today | • Dress them<br>• Feed them breakfast<br>• Get them on the bus |

Duplicate this framework for each of your life goals. As a rule of thumb, you should initially identify 1-3 life goals so that you are thorough without being scattered. You should then identify the tangible objectives that you will accomplish to fulfill the goals. Like the IMS, this LG&O framework should be simply stated but with the deep thought and self-reflection a document of this magnitude requires.

**5) Plan of Action (PoA)**: Now aggregate all your Lifetime Goals & Objectives into a unified Plan of Action (PoA) that clearly shows, in one place, what is required of you.

| Life-Goal 1: *Educate My Children* | | |
|---|---|---|
| **MILESTONE** | **GOAL** | **OBJECTIVES** |
| 30-Year | • Educate my Children at the world's finest universities | • Financing is in Place to Fund four degrees |
| 10-Year | • My Children are all High School Graduates with strong GPAs and varied extra-curricular activities | • All are accepted to universities of their choice |
| 1-Year | • My Children are on a path to becoming well-rounded students | • Spend time tutoring my Children<br>• Enroll them in extra-curricular activities |
| Today | • My children are in school today | • Dress them<br>• Feed them breakfast<br>• Get them on the bus |
| Life-Goal 2: *Raise My Children as a Family* | | |
| **MILESTONE** | **GOAL** | **OBJECTIVES** |
| 30-Year | • My Children interact regularly independent of my Wife and me. | • They plan and execute at least one vacation per year without us. |
| 10-Year | • My Children travel to other cities while we are on vacation together. | • Same country but separate itineraries of my Wife and me. |
| 1-Year | • My Children plan our family vacations together. | • Assign a lead planner<br>• Have them delegate tasks<br>• Supervise |
| Today | • My Children share their treats. | • Give them one Snicker's bar between four Children |
| Life-Goal 3: *Accumulate Enough Money for Running Shoes* | | |
| **MILESTONE** | **GOAL** | **OBJECTIVES** |
| 30-Year | • Successful Business | • Start the business<br>• Work Hard |
| 10-Year | • Masters / Ph.D. | • Keep Working Hard<br>• Select / Apply |
| 1-Year | • Acceptance to College. | • Select<br>• Apply |
| Today | • Work hard today. | • Go in early.<br>• Get home for dinner.<br>• Work when everyone else is asleep. |

**Execution:**

And the first twelve weeks was the easy part. I told you in the beginning this would be hard work – but the really hard work starts now – as you must now go forth and *"Dream by Day"* and make your goals & objectives reality. You can do it! It will be frustrating! But courageously drive on!

**Reviews & Updates:**

**Individuals:** If you are an individual conducting self-development going forward, I suggest you conduct quarterly reviews and annual updates of each of these documents.

**Team Leads:** You should review and update these documents with exactly the same frequency that you provide feedback to your team.

**Corporate Leaders:** Align the reviews and updates with both your Strategic Plan and Human Resources department.

**Begin developing others:**

- **Mentor/Protégé:** Just as someone has taken the time and energy to mentor you in your leadership journey over the past twelve weeks, you should likewise mentor others in their pursuit of Courageous Leadership.
- **Formal Programs:** As stated early on in this book, leadership development is best-delivered through a program. Even as valuable as this twelve weeks of self-development hopefully was for you, and as valuable as your lifelong path to mastery will be for you – your development will be accelerated and enhanced if you participate in more formal programs of development. Concurrently, as a leader, you should consider building and sustaining a leadership development program within your organization. Should you not have the resources to do so internally, you should seek outside resources to assist you. Information on engagement methods can be found at www.FlatterLeadership.com

**Bottom Line Value Creation:**

There is a trick to measuring compound interest known as the *"Rule of 72."* Using this rule with a given interest rate, you can identify how many years an investment will take to double in size.

For example, if you have $100 invested and your investment is earning a return of 7.2%, then it will take ten years to double to $200. That same math applies to your investment in yours or your team's development. If your team is 25% proficient in a particular characteristic and you improve their proficiency by just 10% each year, then their proficiency will double to 50% in 7.2 years. And, with the same rate of improvement, double again to nearly 100% mastery in another 7.2 years. So, with less than 15 years of sustained developmental investment, you can move from relatively low proficiency to near mastery. Said another way, in less than one-half of a typical career, you can move yourself and your team to near mastery in Courageous Leadership.

This explanation is a long way of saying that investment in development will pay off strongly and relatively quickly – for yourself, your team, or your organization. You have invested a great deal in yourself over the past twelve weeks – and would be wise to continue that investment – on your own life-long path to mastering Courageous Leadership.

# Appendix A:

# Templates

- Individual Development     www.FlatterLeadership/IDP
  Plan (IDP):
- Individual Mission     www.FlatterLeadership.com/IMS
  Statement (IMS):
- Journaling Template:     www.FlatterLeadership.com/Journal
- Semi-Structured     www.FlatterLeadership.com/SSC
  Conversations Protocol:
- 12-Week Calendar     www.FlatterLeadership.com/Calendar
- CLC Knowledge Matrix:     www.FlatterLeadership.com/Assessment
- Mentor Request Protocol:     www.FlatterLeadership.com/Mentoring
- Mentor Protégé A.I.R     www.FlatterLeadership.com/AIR
  Protocol:
- Path to Mastery:     www.FlatterLeadership.com/Path

### Developmental Action Templates:

- Principled:     www.FlatterLeadership.com/Principled
- TCE:     www.FlatterLeadership.com/TCE
- WFS:     www.FlatterLeadership.com/WFS
- Vision:     www.FlatterLeadership.com/Visionary
- Humble:     www.FlatterLeadership.com/Humble
- Powerful:     www.FlatterLeadership.com/Bold
- Bold:     www.FlatterLeadership.com/Powerful
- Driven:     www.FlatterLeadership.com/Driven
- Charismatic:     www.FlatterLeadership.com/Charismatic
- Unreasonable:     www.FlatterLeadership.com/Unreasonable

Made in the USA
Lexington, KY
20 June 2018